ACCOUNTABILITY OF THE INTERNATIONAL MONETARY FUND

Voices in Development Management

Series Editor:
Margaret Grieco
Napier University

The Voices in Development Management series provides a forum in which grass roots organisations and development practitioners can voice their views and present their perspectives along with the conventional development experts. Many of the volumes in the series will contain explicit debates between various voices in development and permit the suite of neglected development issues such as gender and transport or the microcredit needs of low income communities to receive appropriate public and professional attention.

Accountability of the International Monetary Fund

Edited by

BARRY CARIN and ANGELA WOOD
Centre for Global Studies, University of Victoria, Canada

International Development Research Centre
Ottawa • Cairo • Dakar • Montevideo • Nairobi • New Delhi • Singapore

ASHGATE

Co-published by

Ashgate Publishing Limited
Gower House
Croft Road
Aldershot
Hampshire GU11 3HR
England

Ashgate Publishing Company
Suite 420
101 Cherry Street
Burlington, VT 05401-4405
USA

International Development Research Centre
PO Box 8500
Ottawa, ON K1G 3H9
Canada
IDRC website: http://www.idrc.ca

Ashgate website: http://www.ashgate.com

British Library Cataloguing in Publication Data
Accountability of the International Monetary Fund. -
(Voices in development management)
1. International Monetary Fund - Officials and employees -
Discipline 2. Liability (Law)
I. Carin, Barry II. Wood, Angela.
332.1'52

Library of Congress Cataloging-in-Publication Data
Carin, Barry, 1946
Accountability of the International Monetary Fund / edited by Barry Carin and Angela Wood.
p. cm. -- (Voices in development management)
Includes bibliographical references and index.
ISBN 0-7546-4523-1
1. International Monetary Fund--Developing countries. 2. International Monetary Fund--Management. 3. International agencies--Decision making. I. Wood, Angela. II. Title. III. Series: University of North London voices in development management.

HG3881.5.I58A333 2005
332.1'52'091724--dc22

2004030373

Ashgate ISBN 0 7546 4523 1
IDRC ISBN 1 55250 175 2

Printed and bound in Great Britain by TJ International Ltd, Padstow, Cornwall

Contents

Preface

Accountability is a multi-dimensional concept. Most simply put, it involves decision makers being held responsible for the decisions they take. This simple definition raises many questions: who should be involved in the decision making process, how should decisions be taken, and who should hold decision makers to account? Other questions include: what degree of transparency should there be regarding decisions taken, against what criteria should decision makers be judged, and what mechanisms and processes are needed to facilitate holding decision makers to account? The intent of this volume is to further inform the debate on some of these issues in relation to the accountability of the International Monetary Fund (IMF) to its various stakeholders.

The Executive Board

One of the central failings of the IMF's current governance structure is the lack of effective participation by many of the developing countries, Sub-Saharan African countries in particular, in the decision making processes of the Executive Board. As Rustomjee reveals in Chapter 1, the skewed allocation of votes and board seats in favour of the richest countries undermines consensus decision making. Little opportunity is provided for the developing countries to put their concerns on to the board's agenda or to get their views taken into account during board discussions. The implication is that the priorities of the IMF do not necessarily reflect those of the majority of the institution's clients, that is, those members who borrow from the IMF, and that decisions taken may not be optimal because they do not consider borrowers' needs or capacities. This lack of understanding leads to a loss of ownership and instances of poor policy and program design, and ultimately can lead to policy and program failure.

Furthermore, developing country Executive Directors (EDs) assume a disproportionate share of the workload since they typically represent more members who are engaged in IMF programs. Relatively speaking, developing country EDs are less well resourced, have less institutional memory and face greater intra-constituency political and coordination challenges, all of which further limits their ability to engage optimally in the board.

Rustomjee's proposed solution is firstly to initiate a dialogue on the issue of developing country representation, either by: 1) establishing a committee of the Executive Board reporting to the governors; 2) establishing a committee of the Board of Governors; or 3) carrying out an external review.

Secondly, he proposes several options for increasing the voting share of all or a subset of developing countries, while maintaining an assured but not excessive majority of the voting power for creditor countries. Options include:

reallocating votes between developed and developing countries, increasing the basic vote, and using purchasing power parity (PPP) as a means of calculating gross domestic product (GDP) in the quota formula.

Thirdly, Rustomjee calls for the creation of one or two additional seats for Sub-Saharan African countries and possibly an additional Asian seat, either by increasing the size of the board, or reducing the number of seats held by European countries.

Finally, he proposes to increase the length of terms for elected EDs to be between three and five years to address the challenge of institutional memory constraints, and to increase the number of staff in their offices to account for the relative intensity of their workload.

The Role of National Parliaments

Eggers, Florini, and Woods find in Chapter 2 that parliaments are paying more attention to the activities of the IMF through oversight mechanisms and by influencing policy decisions. In some developing countries, parliaments have rejected IMF reform proposals, leading the IMF to put much more effort into consulting and persuading program country parliaments. Some developing country parliaments are also looking to finds ways to systematically become proactive, rather than merely reacting to IMF-Executive Branch agreements post hoc.

Parliamentary engagement with the IMF will remain limited unless both the IMF and national governments at least permit, if not facilitate or require, parliaments to get involved. Although parliaments ought to be among the key stakeholders included in the Poverty Reduction Strategy process, the IMF's Articles of Agreement limit its negotiating remit to the finance ministry and central bank governors. There is an obvious role for the IMF to play in informing, explaining and communicating information about economic policy to parliaments. However, currently there is much scepticism among parliamentarians about the impartiality of the Fund's efforts in this regard.

The IMF's effort to improve transparency is a vital step towards democratic accountability and needs to be further encouraged. If parliaments are effectively to hold the IMF to account, it is vital that they know whether it is the board or the management and staff they should be holding to account for a particular decision or policy. This demands greater transparency and duty to disclose at the board level. One option is to require a formal vote on all issues and to keep and publish the voting record.

Enhancing Learning and Policy Accountability

In Chapter 3, Wood argues that since individual IMF staff or board members cannot be held accountable for policy outcomes, it is not legitimate for the IMF to impose policy choices on government institutions through conditionality.

Governments should be responsible for policy choices, have ownership of them, and therefore be accountable to their electorates for their outcomes. However, the IMF continues to have an important advisory role to play since developing countries do need a good and reliable source of macroeconomic advice.

The quality of the IMF's advice is not always as high as it should be since it has neglected to develop effective monitoring and evaluation systems to facilitate evidence-based policy making. As a result there is an absence of a learning culture in the IMF which leads to instances of poor policy advice.

Wood advocates the introduction of a participatory systematic learning process based on prior assessment of anticipated policy outcomes and risks, monitoring of intermediate outcomes during implementation, and evaluation of actual – in relation to anticipated – outcomes on completion. Such a system needs to be transparent and complemented with performance-related staff incentives. Transparency could be improved by making public the IMF's database on the monitoring of arrangements (MONA) and producing an annual report on program performance.

Staff incentives should be reoriented to discourage rapid department switching, and to reward staff for developing country-based knowledge and for improvements in policy outcome forecasting. The Policy Development and Review department's screening of program content should be reoriented so as not to discourage policy innovation. When hiring staff, greater priority should be given to candidates with experience in policy application.

Operational Policies and Procedures, and an Ombudsman

Bradlow, in Chapter 4, argues that the number and range of actors with which the IMF is engaged has grown beyond the point where its operating practices can be kept informal and known only by a relatively small number of experts. Consequently, it needs to develop a set of operational policies and procedures to guide its interactions with a broader range of stakeholders and to guide its decision making. Indeed, the IMF is unusual in that it has not already done so.

The benefits include: providing effective guidance for staff when conducting their work; predictability in the conduct of IMF operations; transparency in IMF decision making and action; promotion of accountability; and facilitated learning. The costs include: increased bureaucratisation; loss of flexibility; and possible disincentives to innovation. However, on balance, the benefits are greater. Such procedures will allow outside stakeholders to engage more effectively with the IMF, public understanding of the IMF's operations will be improved, they will promote accountability, and internal governance will be improved.

In order for operational policies and procedures to be effective, they need to be supported by a mechanism capable of monitoring and promoting compliance with them. Bradlow concludes that the mechanism best suited to the IMF is an independent ombudsman with the authority to investigate complaints from directly affected people and groups about staff and management non-compliance with the policies and procedures.

Acknowledgement

The Centre for Global Studies acknowledges the generous support of the Ford Foundation.

List of Abbreviations

BP	Bank Procedures
CAE	Country Assistance Evaluations
CAO	Compliance Advisor Ombudsman
CDF	Comprehensive Development Framework
DFID	Department for International Development
ECLAC	Economic Commission for Latin America and the Caribbean
ED	Executive Directors
ESAF	Enhanced Structural Adjustment Facility
FAO	Food and Agricultural Organization of the United Nations
GDP	Gross domestic product
GP	Good Practices
HIPC	Heavily Indebted Poor Countries
IBRD	International Bank for Reconstruction and Development
IDA	International Development Association
IEO	Independent Evaluation Office
IFC	International Finance Corporation
IFI	International Financial Institutions
IMF	International Monetary Fund
MDBs	Multilateral Development Banks
MDG	Millennium Development Goals
MIGA	Multilateral Investment Guarantee Agency
MONA	Monitoring of arrangement
MPIA	Macroeconomic Policy Impact Assessment
NEPAD	New Partnership for Africa's Development
NGO	Non-governmental Organization
OECD	Organization for Economic Co-operation and Development
OED	Operations Evaluation Department
OIA	Office of Internal Audit and Inspection (IMF)
OD	Operational Directives
OP	Operational Policies
Op. Memos	Operational Memos
PDR	Policy Development and Review Department (IMF)
PIN	Public Information Notice
PIW	Project Implementation Watch
PNoWB	Parliamentary Network on the World Bank
PPP	Purchasing power parity
PRGF	Poverty Reduction Growth Facility
PRS	Poverty Reduction Strategy
PRSP	Poverty Reduction Strategy Paper
PSIA	Poverty and Social Impact Analysis

SDR	Special Drawing Rights
SPA	Special Partnership with Africa
SSA	Sub-Saharan African Countries
UN	United Nations
UNICEF	United Nations Children's Fund
UNIFEM	United Nations Development Fund for Women
UNDP	United Nations Development Programme
UNCTAD	United Nations Conference on Trade and Development
WHO	World Health Organization
WTO	World Trade Organization

Introduction

Angela Wood

The International Monetary Fund's (IMF) growing influence and role in developing countries has generated demands for greater accountability. Moreover, as a larger number of people have become affected by its policy advice, demands have grown for the IMF to consult with and be more accountable to a wider range of stakeholders, both inside and outside governments.

Accountability means that decisions taken should be predictable, equitable, based on sound judgement, follow clear and enforceable procedures, and have clear mechanisms for reporting. Those responsible for taking decisions should be answerable for them to clearly defined authorities. The problem for the IMF is that although its role and policy reach, the potential impact of its policies, and its client base has changed considerably since it was founded, the mechanisms by which decisions are taken and who takes them have not. In addition there is considerable murkiness as to who should be responsible for these decisions and to whom. As a result, the IMF's own accountability does not reach the standards of transparency and good governance that it demands of its members.

The IMF's transformation has been rapid since the 1970s when the collapse of the Gold Standard fixed exchange rate system gave way to flexible exchange rates and ended the IMF's original purpose of maintaining exchange rate alignment. By the mid 1980s the IMF had turned its attention to addressing the Latin American debt problems through structural adjustment. In the early 1990s it was thrust into the role of helping to develop market-based economies in the countries of the Former Soviet Union, and by the end of the decade it was dealing with financial sector reform and systemic financial crises. Today, in the poorest countries, it is engaged in establishing the macroeconomic conditions for poverty reduction. The changing role of the institution has led it deeper into more areas of domestic policy making. It has increasingly focused on restructuring borrowing countries' economic systems and latterly public institutions as well.

As the IMF's role has changed, so too has its client base. The membership has increased from the original 45 to 184 countries today. This reflects the change in the political landscape as developing countries have achieved independence from former colonial rulers and the Soviet Union has been dismantled. These new clients are more economically diverse and have a wider range of needs and priorities than the original membership.

While previously the IMF operated as a credit union, with all members likely to borrow from it from time to time, today the IMF has structural creditors and structural debtors. The creditors, the developed countries, are highly unlikely to actually borrow from the IMF, and prefer to borrow directly from private markets free from the policy interference of the IMF. The debtors, the developing countries, in some cases borrow almost continuously from the IMF and must submit to its policy demands. Today, the IMF's program work is wholly conducted in the developing and emerging market countries.

Despite these significant changes, the systems by which the IMF is governed and decisions taken have not evolved and continue to be based on original divisions of power. Many of the poorest countries, which are most regularly in discussion with the IMF about debt relief and structural adjustment programs, are barely represented in the IMF's decision making structures – the Executive Board and the International Monetary and Finance Committee. A larger proportion of board seats are held by developed countries than developing countries. The distribution of votes, which is allocated according to a country's strength in the world economy, is also heavily skewed in favour of the richest countries.

This means that the developed countries can dominate board decision making and it is almost impossible for developing countries to put their priorities on to the IMF's agenda, which the principal shareholders continue to set. As a consequence, a yawning gap has developed between the institution's stakeholders and shareholders, and those who are affected by decisions and those who should be accountable for them. The problem is that the developed country decision makers are largely unaffected by the decisions they take. This not only undermines the legitimacy of the decisions taken, it potentially affects their quality. The implication is that because the developing countries' views are not taken into consideration, the board's decisions are sometimes less than optimal.

Similarly, a lack of engagement between the IMF staff and a broad range of national stakeholders has the potential to negatively affect the quality of the IMF's advice to governments. Despite the depth of the IMF's influence in domestic policy making, the IMF's engagement with national stakeholders still remains largely confined to the finance minister, central bank governor and sometimes the head of government. This lack of participation and open discussion undermines transparency. Furthermore, finance ministers are increasingly entering into agreements with the IMF about policy choices beyond the finance ministry's remit and outside the country's political process. This means that they cannot effectively be held accountable at the national level. Since the IMF holds the purse strings and access to IMF resources is often vital, the tendency has been for the finance ministry to listen and be accountable to the IMF rather than to its fellow ministers and citizens.

Within the IMF, identifying who should be held to account, for what and by whom, is not always immediately clear. There are several layers of decision making and many voices in the decision making process. When deciding on program content and policy advice, the staff's technical judgements may be mixed with the board's political concerns. The IMF's institutional priorities and responsibilities are decided by a small group of governors, overseen by the Executive Board, and carried out by the staff.

The IMF's hierarchy is clear: IMF staff and management are accountable to the Managing Director, who is appointed by and accountable to the Executive

Board, which in turn is appointed by and accountable to the Board of Governors, which is appointed by and is ultimately accountable to the member states. But there are problems at every level, which impedes the effectiveness of oversight.

Firstly, the staff and management have far superior information than the Executive Board, which is supposed to oversee the day-to-day management of the IMF. Therefore, the staff has relative autonomy, except perhaps in relation to the largest shareholders. There is a tendency for the board to simply 'rubber stamp' programs presented to them by the management. Moreover, since the distribution of board votes is heavily skewed in favour of a handful of creditor countries, staff and management accountability tends to be biased towards the preferences of these countries. The fact that the Managing Director is chosen by the European members and the Deputy Managing Director by the US government is also likely to reinforce this tendency.

Secondly, at the board level most countries are grouped into constituencies. In some constituencies the appointment of the Executive Director (ED), who makes decisions on the constituency's behalf at the board, is rotated amongst the membership and in others the country with the largest number of votes appoints the ED. Unless a government actually has the chair and gets to appoint its own ED, in most cases it has relatively little influence over the positions taken by the ED and by and large it has little means to hold the ED and therefore the staff and management to account.

Thirdly, while the buck should finally come to rest with the Board of Governors, which is comprised mostly of finance ministers and in some cases central bank governors, it has little ability to effectively oversee the institution's activities. The governors' engagement in the IMF is only partial. They meet only once a year, and except for those who are elected to the International Monetary and Finance Committee (membership of the committee is based on the same constituency system as the Executive Board), which meets only twice a year, their role is largely cosmetic.

Fourthly, there is the question of who holds the finance minister or central bank governor to account and how accountability at this level can be metered out. Ideally, this should be the responsibility of parliaments. At present, parliamentarians, especially in developing countries, typically have little knowledge of the IMF and little access to information about the governor and ED's engagement in it. There is an absence of formal, recorded voting procedures and vital information about ED's positions regarding board decisions is not made public. Moreover, in the case of many of the poorest countries, their ED has so little influence in the decision making process that it becomes almost meaningless to try to hold him/her to account. Yet parliamentarians in developing countries have no means of holding other board members or governors to account. Nor can IMF staff or management be held accountable at the national level since as members of an international institution they have legal immunity and cannot be held accountable even by a national court of law. Given the usually indirect links to the IMF's decision making structures, there may be few incentives for members of parliament to involve themselves in overseeing the IMF's activities.

This accountability void may be filled in part by non-governmental organisations, which often seek accountability directly from the IMF leaving aside the parliamentary process, but there are no formal mechanisms for doing so. Although individual staff and EDs have made significant effort to engage more with civil society, this engagement is typically ad hoc and expectations are unclear. The result is that, often, civil society organisations remain unsatisfied with the outcome of interactions. Moreover, for civil society in the developing countries a lack of resources, a lack of information, or an inability to organise can limit their capacity to exercise informal oversight, although capacity is improving. Ultimately this means that there is no requirement for IMF staff or management to be directly accountable to citizens in program countries, nor is there much likelihood that the governor or ED will be held accountable either.

While the crux of the accountability problem lies in the inadequate representation of members on the Executive Board, particularly those governments who borrow from the IMF, and the distance of the board from those who are affected by IMF policies, there is also a lack of mechanisms through which oversight and accountability takes place.

Internally, review and accountability is confined to the Office of Internal Audit and Inspection (OIA) and the Policy Development and Review department (PDR). The OIA's remit is confined to reviewing the IMF's organisational and operational effectiveness and auditing the Fund's accounts. Reports are made to the board, but are not published. PDR is responsible for ensuring consistency between programs and countries' equitable treatment, although no formal procedures exist. All policy and operational documents, program related documents, mission briefs and reports, and surveillance reports pass through PDR for clearance before they are submitted for approval by the Managing Director, and finally by the board. PDR also conducts sporadic evaluations of policies and program outcomes in relation to objectives, but these are not linked to any mechanism of accountability and are not necessarily made public. There is potentially a moral hazard problem in that PDR staff both establishes policies and programs and reviews them without any external input into the process. There is no systematic monitoring or reporting of program outcomes, unlike at the World Bank where all completed projects are reviewed by its Operations Evaluation Department and an annual report is published. Neither is staff performance monitored nor are staff incentives linked to performance in relation to core IMF objectives.

Although there is much missing in terms of a coherent system of accountability, the IMF has made efforts in recent years, some considerable, to address some of its critics' concerns. Since 1999, the IMF has produced a few new operational policies and guidelines for staff. Most notable perhaps are those that were the culmination of the conditionality streamlining process embarked upon in 2001. The process called for greater transparency and clarity as to what constitutes conditionality but also called for a scaling back of the number of conditions and the areas to which conditionality would be applied. However, operational policies and guidelines remain few, covering only a small area of the staff's work. Apart from reports to the board prepared by the staff there is as yet no formal mechanism to regularly monitor compliance or allow external stakeholders to raise complaints where non-compliance is suspected.

In 2001 the IMF established the Independent Evaluation Office (IEO), which undertakes ad hoc evaluations and reports directly to the Executive Board. Its reports, which are made public, have proved useful for prompting reflection and operational change in the IMF, although it does not operate explicitly as an accountability mechanism (preferring to focus on learning) and it is not a vehicle through which external stakeholders can participate or pursue complaints.

Since 1999 there has been a marked increase in transparency, which makes accountability to external stakeholders more effective, as well as making it clearer what the IMF can be held accountable for. The IMF has revised its policies on making program and surveillance documents, staff reports, and its archives public. There is now a much stronger presumption of publication although it is still not yet mandatory. Nor are internal reviews automatically made public. More importantly, although the introduction of Chairman's Summaries and Public Information Notices summarising board discussions on country programs, surveillance reports, and broad policy issues is welcome, the lack of transparency surrounding board decision making and the positions taken by individual board members continues to impede accountability to member states and citizens.

Finally, in 1999 the IMF established a committee to review its quota formula, which determines how much each country must pay into the IMF and therefore each country's allocation of votes. In 2000 the IMF established a joint committee with the World Bank to examine the processes by which the IMF Managing Director and World Bank President are selected. Revealingly, both of these processes were conducted under a very limited remit and to no substantive effect.

Although these steps towards improved transparency, evaluation and ownership are welcome, they are only the first towards a coherent system of accountability. By themselves they do not create accountability, but they offer a useful foundation from which to build better structures and processes. This discussion makes clear that there are many aspects of IMF accountability that need to be addressed and the complex relations require clarification and simplification. New systems need to be introduced and old governance structures need to be modified. Some of the apparently most pressing issues, such as voting and board reform, may be the most difficult to address since they will require the willing surrender of power. This report does not try to address all of the issues raised here. Rather, a pragmatic approach is taken to look at several key issues that could be practically implemented within current constraints.

One of the most urgent issues is how to achieve better representation of developing countries on the Executive Board. The inability of developing country EDs to adequately represent the views of their constituency members at the board is explored in Chapter 1. Cyrus Rustomjee shows how a lack of voting power prohibits developing country governments from putting forward their opinions to the board. The result is weaker, and sometimes inappropriate, board decisions which can hamper progress in developing countries. At best developing country governments can be reactive to the agendas of the developed countries but they have almost no opportunity to propose their own agenda. The inability of developing country EDs to be proactive is further undermined by the burden of work they shoulder in terms of representing their clients, an issue starkly demonstrated by the case of the two Sub-Saharan African EDs. Rustomjee considers several options for increasing developing countries' capacity to engage more fully and effectively in board discussions.

There is very clearly an extremely weak link between most member governments, the Executive Board and the IMF management and staff. Andrew Eggers, Ann Florini and Ngaire Woods explore in Chapter 2 what options and limitations there are for parliamentarians to become more involved in oversight of the Executive Board as the legitimate interlocutor between civil society and government.

In Chapter 3, Angela Wood argues that the demand for greater accountability arises from the perceived failure of the IMF to learn from its policy shortcomings and to take account of the risks to full policy implementation. Wood explores the limitations for holding the IMF staff directly to account for the outcomes of its policy advice. She suggests that it would be more productive to focus less on apportioning blame and to pay more attention to adopting mechanisms to improve policy advice and enhance staff learning. Wood argues that accountability can be effectively demonstrated by putting lessons learned into practice. Wood outlines the core components and process of a systematic learning mechanism and argues that for such a process to be useful, it needs to be complemented with appropriate incentive structures and transparency mechanisms.

Staff and management are not held directly accountable for the outcomes of their policy advice. Daniel Bradlow makes the case in Chapter 4 for formal operational policies and procedures. With these, affected peoples can hold the IMF staff to account for how they conduct their work and go about making decisions. A mechanism to investigate claims of non-compliance is necessary. Bradlow compares the current relative lack of operational policies and procedures, and mechanisms for enforcing them at the IMF with the situation in the multilateral development banks. He evaluates the feasibility of establishing a comprehensive set of operational policies and procedures, and considers the case for establishing a mechanism for holding the staff and management accountable for compliance with them. Finally, he identifies the key features of a compliance mechanism.

Chapter 1

Improving Southern Voice on the IMF Board: Quo Vadis Shareholders?

Cyrus Rustomjee[1]

Introduction

There is a growing and persuasive body of literature to suggest that the voice of developing countries in the International Monetary Fund (IMF) should be significantly improved. Several of these studies focus on the improvements which can be made to the internal functioning of the institution, in ways that favour the interests of developing countries.[2] Others focus more directly on the options for improving developing countries' representation, or voice, in the IMF Executive Board itself.[3] Yet however clear the argument, the obstacles to achieving these objectives are very significant indeed. Meaningful changes can only be made with the consent of the industrial countries, which hold a majority of the voting power in the IMF Executive Board and of course in the IMF Board of Governors. And these members currently see little benefit in changing the status quo. This, in turn, presents an additional challenge: to identify processes which can unlock the current impasse between developing and industrial countries – largely represented by debtors and creditors respectively, on the issue of improved developing country influence in the decision making processes of the IMF Executive Board.

This chapter focuses on the challenge of improving the voice of developing countries on the IMF board, given their inadequate representation. The presumption is that creditors in the IMF Executive Board should, particularly in regard to financing decisions, maintain an assured majority of the voting power. It examines some of the recent literature on developing country representation in the

---

[1] The author would wish to thank the Ford Foundation for the grant which made it possible for the paper to be produced; and the University of Natal, South Africa, where the author is an Honorary Research Fellow, for facilities provided.

[2] See for example Evans and Finnemore (2001), who provide a detailed treatment of potential organisational reforms which could significantly strengthen the voice of developing countries in the IMF. These proposals briefly touch on options to increase the voice of developing countries in the IMF Executive Board itself, but also focus on other options, including rebalancing resources and obligations in area departments; decentralising staffing; increasing mid-career hiring to attract staff with direct experience in developing countries; and sub-contracting research to developing country researchers.

[3] See for example Buira (2002); Bradlow (2001); and Mohammed (2002).

board and seeks to identify some options for improving such representation. This literature points broadly to the presence and the deepening of two parallel challenges which currently confront the collective membership of the institution.

The first challenge is a decline in the efficiency of conduct of board work, focusing on the long-term disadvantages of its imbalanced decision making arrangements. The argument is that inefficient representation arrangements are leading to less than optimal decision making based on a failure to adequately understand the needs of the majority of the institution's clients. The inadequate understanding leads to instances of poor policy and program design; and ultimately in some instances to policy and program failure. The costs of this challenge are significant and direct, both to the institution as a whole and to the members concerned.

The second challenge is that the representation arrangements for developing countries in the IMF Executive Board have now become so unbalanced that there is a substantive claim that the overall representation process is no longer democratic and does not promote the principles of consensus, cooperation, collaboration and multilateralism upon which the IMF was founded.

Change is solely the responsibility of the shareholders of the IMF. If there are to be changes that improve the developing country representation, these cannot come from IMF management and staff, but will need to occur through decisions taken by the shareholders of the institution, in practice through decisions of the Board of Governors. Prima facie, this appears to make the task of addressing these challenges all the more complex.

The recent conclusion of the Twelfth Quota Review process resulted in a decision not to increase quotas and hence passed up an opportunity to make corrections in the quota arrangements – and therefore relative voting power in the board. This decision highlights the considerable inertia in the quota and voting process and the reluctance of the largest shareholders to make changes to quota and voting arrangements.[4] But as Buira and other commentators note, there are now powerful economic and political reasons for changes in representation arrangements which favour developing countries.[5] These arguments are growing and it would be opportune to find mechanisms for open and detailed discussion of the various options that could be considered in any rearrangement of board representation. Doing so will contribute to strengthening governance, addressing the concerns of a large segment of the IMF's membership, and could reveal some options which limit the adverse economic and political impacts perceived by some creditors.

The second part of this chapter outlines the scope of the challenge confronting developing countries, in view of the current system of weighted voting, coupled with the current distribution of board seats among the membership. The third part sets out a case for improving the representation of developing countries in the board. Developing country interests are to a large extent

---

[4] Refer to IMF (2003): Press Release No. 03/02: IMF board Recommends to Governors Conclusion of Quota Review, IMF, Washington DC.

[5] See Buira (2002).

homogeneous and their claims for strengthened representation are largely based on a common set of arguments. This section outlines three key arguments for an early improvement in the status of developing countries in the board. It also presents some of the specific arguments raised by sub-groups among developing countries. The third part examines some of the arguments why developing countries are currently in so unfavourable a position, and concludes with some potential considerations that could point to a way forward.

The fourth part of the chapter illustrates the general claim for stronger developing country representation by focusing on the representation arrangements for one large section of the IMF's membership, Sub-Saharan African countries (SSA) – one quarter of the IMF's member countries – the most significantly affected by the imbalanced representation arrangements in the Executive Board. The fifth part suggests a range of options and proposals for change in representation arrangements that can begin to address the twin challenges of strengthening efficiency and strengthening of democratic process. Part six concludes.

Voting Share and Board Presence – the Status Quo

The magnitude of the challenge confronting developing countries in seeking to improve their status in the IMF Executive Board is formidable. There are two basic benchmarks for assessing the legitimacy of developing countries' claims for a stronger voice relative to their power in the board. Firstly, voting share; and secondly the share of board seats. In combination, they present an accurate reflection of the influence of developing countries in the Executive Board.

Determining Relative Voting Share – Two Approaches

One approach assigns the voting shares of each individual member to a specific category (for example emerging market, Heavily Indebted Poor Countries (HIPC), transitional and other countries) and aggregates the voting shares in each category. The second approach examines voting share on a constituency basis, based on the current distribution of Executive Board seats. Each approach has advantages and disadvantages. The category-based approach provides an accurate reflection of the precise voting share of categories such as emerging markets, or of developing countries as a whole. However, it does not take account of the fact that Executive Directors are not permitted to split their votes and to cast separate votes for each of the members they represent. Instead, they are required to cast a single block vote for all of their members. The second approach, which focuses on the constituencies as a whole, recognises the reality of board voting practice, but masks the fact that some constituencies, which are headed by creditor members, may also represent debtor countries.

A comprehensive example of the former approach is provided in Evans and Finnemore (2001). This approach reveals that developing countries, comprising the emerging market economies, HIPC and Non-HIPC Poverty

Reduction Growth Facility (PRGF) countries, India, China and a number of other developing countries, hold approximately 30.3 per cent of the voting share in the Executive Board. A further 8.2 per cent is held by the transitional and other countries, including, in Evans and Finnemore's methodology, the Russian Federation. By contrast, the G-7, the Netherlands, Belgium and Sweden hold a majority of 51.5 per cent. When combined with all other OECD countries, the creditor members of the institution hold a majority of 61.45 per cent of the total vote.

A second approach to assessing relative voting strength is to examine voting based on the current constituencies in the board. The collective voting strength of the Executive Directors from developing countries, together with the number of developing country Executive Directors is illustrated in Table 1.1. The table highlights the fact that, based on the current configuration of the Executive Board, there are eleven Executive Directors whose constituencies are headed by developing country members, almost all of whom are debtors. Ten of the available 24 board seats are occupied by developing countries and collectively these members hold 26.2 per cent of the voting share. Note that the number of developing country board seats rises to eleven seats when the constituency currently headed by Spain is chaired by Mexico or Venezuela.[6]

On the above analysis of voting power, if joined by the Russian Federation, a single country constituency which has been an important debtor member in recent years, the developing country group holds a voting share of just under 29 per cent. This aggregate falls considerably short of a simple majority of the voting power, which is the minimum required for any decision of the Executive Board. For developing countries to be able to carry a decision in their favour, they must build alliances with creditor members.

Table 1.1 IMF Executive Board: voting share and distribution of board seats

Country/Constituency	**Total Constituency Voting Share (%)**
1. Chairs Headed By Creditor Members	
US	17.10
Japan	6.14
Germany	6.00
France	4.95
UK	4.95
Italy	4.19
Canada	3.71
Total G-7	**47.04**

[6] Each constituency has its internal rules, among its members, for board representation. In the case of the seat currently chaired by Spain, a rotation arrangement is in place which enables Mexico, Spain and Venezuela to rotate the constituency chair.

Country/Constituency	**Total Constituency Voting Share (%)**
Belgium	5.14
Netherlands	4.85
Iceland	3.51
Total G-10	**60.54**
Spain	4.28
Australia	3.33
Switzerland	2.85
Total Creditor Group	**71.00**
2. Chairs Headed By Developing Country Members	
Saudi Arabia	3.23
Indonesia	3.18
Nigeria	3.18
Egypt	2.95
China	2.94
Brazil	2.46
Iran	2.45
India	2.40
Chile	2.00
Equatorial Guinea	1.41
Total Developing Country Group	**26.20**
Russian Federation	2.75
Total Debtor Group	**28.95**

Source: IMF Voting Shares – IMF Website: www.imf.org.

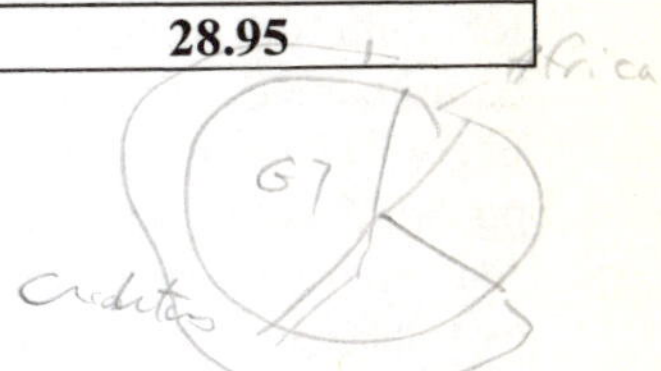

The Influence of Mixed Constituencies

In addition to the ten constituencies almost entirely comprised of developing country debtors, there are also currently eight mixed constituencies, containing both creditor and debtor members. These comprise the constituencies currently headed by Italy, Canada, Belgium, the Netherlands, Iceland, Spain, Australia and Switzerland. Of these, all of the above-cited countries, except Iceland and Spain, permanently head their constituencies, with Iceland rotating its constituency chair with a small group of Nordic members and Spain rotating its constituency chair with Venezuela and Mexico. For these mixed constituencies, one proxy to assess the likely degree to which a particular constituency would support a developing country position in the process of decision making is the relative share of voting power among debtors and creditors within each mixed constituency.[7] Using this approach, the following table illustrates the creditor share of the total voting power in each of these constituencies.

Table 1.2 Creditor/debtor voting share in mixed constituencies

Mixed Constituency Headed By	Creditor Share of Total Constituency Vote (%)
Italy	96.9
Canada	90.0
Iceland	94.6
Belgium	61.1
Netherlands	58.3
Australia	57.7
Switzerland	56.3
Spain	33.1

Source: Data From IMF Voting Shares, IMF Website: www.imf.org, May 2003.

The table illustrates that in seven of the eight mixed creditor/debtor constituencies, the majority of voting power resides with creditors. In the cases of the constituencies chaired by Italy, Canada, and Iceland, creditors are in the overwhelming majority by voting power. This means that even if all five remaining mixed constituencies were to favour a position supported by developing countries, and even if the Russian Federation opted to join this decision, these members would not be able to muster a simple majority of voting power.

Among the remaining five mixed constituencies, there is varying scope for building alliances with developing countries. Clearly, of all the mixed constituencies, the constituency currently chaired by Spain is considered most likely to cast its vote in favour of developing countries. With its cooperation, the potential voting power of developing countries as a whole increases to 33.2 per cent. If Australia, which represents a series of Asia-Pacific countries, were to also cast its vote in favour of developing countries, the potential voting power of developing countries as a whole would increase to 36.6 per cent.[8] This again

[7] This is a useful general proxy, although it should be noted that on many occasions, particularly in regard to country matters, each of the eight mixed constituencies have at times taken positions favoring developing countries.

[8] In practice, the extent of such cooperation with developing countries, by the mixed constituencies containing both debtor and creditor members, hinges on the nature of the

remains well short of a simple majority of the voting power. For all these reasons, it seems clear that on an issue on which creditors and debtors are significantly divided, it is likely, based on the above analysis, that seven of the eight mixed constituencies would vote in favour of creditor interests.

Conclusion: Relative Voting Share

The tables above indicate that developing countries have a minority of seats in the IMF board and hold approximately 29 per cent of the voting share. Chairs represented by creditors currently enjoy approximately 71 per cent of the voting share. There are eight mixed constituencies, with varying degrees of creditor/debtor mix. If some of these mixed constituencies opt to vote in favour of developing country interests, the share of the vote in favour of developing country positions rises accordingly. There are indeed numerous examples of individual mixed constituency members 'breaking rank' and voting in favour of a debtor position in the board. However, the large bulk of these occur in regard to the details of country-specific programmes and not in respect of policy issues; and almost never by means of a collective shift in vote by all mixed constituencies. With creditor interests dominant in three of the eight mixed constituencies, there is no realistic prospect of developing countries assembling an alliance of board members in favour of an explicitly debtor position.

The aggregates in Table 1.1 also reveal a further challenge for developing countries: whereas the aggregate voting share of creditor members is 61.45 per cent (per the methodology used by Evans and Finnemore, 2001), the voting share which creditor members can muster, because of the practice of voting as an entire constituency, can rise to 66.7 per cent.[9] This is in excess of the aggregate voting share of creditor members.

Additional Challenges for Developing Countries

Aside from the consequences of the current delineation of constituencies in the IMF Executive Board for relative voting power, there are other additional consequences of the current delineation which favour creditor members. The first of these is that developing country Executive Directors tend to assume a disproportionately large share of the workload associated with the representation function in the board; not only do they represent on average several more members than most creditor members, but they represent members with financing programmes with the IMF, which many of the creditor members do not. The contrast is most clearly illustrated in comparing the respective responsibilities of the single-country creditor constituencies, particularly five of the G-7: the USA,

---

policy or financing program under discussion. This occurs particularly in the case of country programs.

[9] This excludes the votes cast by the Spanish Executive Director. If the latter constituency were to cast its vote in favour of a creditor position, the share of voting power which creditors could muster increases to 71 per cent.

Japan, Germany, France and the United Kingdom. All of these countries are single country constituencies with some large developing country constituencies, which represent over twenty members, a large proportion of which have IMF-funded programmes.

The challenge of a disproportionate workload is compounded by two further factors. Firstly, the large industrial members are better resourced and generally better informed. This decisively influences the representation function. Developing country members, because of their broader country representation responsibilities, are obliged to spread resources more thinly. They do not enjoy the extensive institutional support provided by their constituency member countries; and as they represent several members, they are obliged to address coordination and intra-constituency political challenges which the single country creditor constituencies do not.

The second factor is that the mechanism which has sought to address these different challenges among the membership – the process of staffing Executive Directors' offices – has tended not to keep pace with the expansion of the IMF's role in developing countries. Staffing arrangements do offer some compensation, by linking the number of staff in constituency offices with the number of countries represented. However this approach should be bolstered for three reasons:

- Firstly, staff arrangements take no account of the intensity of programme relationships, for example whether a member has a financing programme or not; whether the member's programme is in difficulty; whether particular relations attach, for example the fact that a member may be a large emerging market economy either in or about to enter into a crisis, or the fact that a member may, in addition to having a PRGF arrangement, also be an HIPC-eligible member.
- Secondly, staffing arrangements have also tended not to take account of the significant diseconomies of scale which arise with constituency representation in the case of large multi-country constituencies, particularly those with large numbers of IMF-supported programmes.
- Thirdly, the expansion of the IMF's work in developing countries in recent decades has significantly outstripped the staffing resources provided to the constituency offices.

A further challenge for developing country Executive Directors focuses on the term of office. This has tended to favour, albeit inadvertently, the creditor members and particularly the appointed Executive Directors. The multi-country nature of constituency representation has meant that in some instances, developing country Executive Directors have tended to remain for shorter periods in the Executive Board, being obliged to yield the chair to other members of the constituency. In part this has been attributable to internal rules within constituencies; and in part this has been attributable to the fact that Executive Directors' elections take place every two years. A lengthening of the terms of service of Executive Directors, for example by holding elections every three or four years, would tend to favour the elective constituencies, by strengthening institutional memory in these constituencies and enabling developing country Executive Directors to have a strengthened influence on decision making, by enabling these individuals to benefit from greater familiarity with board policies and procedures because of their longer terms of service.

Arguments for Improving Developing Country Voice

Common Concerns of All Developing Countries

There are three equally forceful sets of arguments. Firstly, the need for strengthened voting share and board presence due to the increased level of involvement of the IMF in developing countries in recent decades.[10] Indeed, the claims of developing countries for strengthened representation have grown in recent years, in tandem with the growing influence in the global economy of the large emerging market economies and the transition economies and with the IMF's significantly increased role in low-income countries. Secondly, the need to restore what has become a significant departure from the principle of effective consensus-based decision making and a drift toward simple majority decision making. And thirdly, decision making in respect of the interests of developing countries has tended to become unnecessarily poor and unbalanced.

(i) Increased level of involvement of the IMF in developing countries
The IMF's work in developing countries has expanded significantly in each of the last three decades, to the extent that developing countries now account for by far the largest client base of the institution. Developing countries are the focus of the significant majority of the IMF's policies, the entirety of the institution's financing, almost all of its technical assistance and a large part of IMF surveillance activity. The quantum of resources now provided by the IMF to its members has significantly increased in recent years.[11]

---

[10] Note that it has been nearly three decades since IMF financial resources were used by a large industrial country.

[11] Successive IMF Annual Reports since 1995 reveal that the increase has taken place in respect of the IMF's regular resources, as well as the PRGF. The IMF Annual Report for 2002, for example, notes that in 2001, augmentations of existing arrangements and new arrangements contributed to a sharp rise in new IMF commitments in the IMF's Financial Year 2002, p. 57. The same report also notes that the IMF committed new PRGF loan resources of US$2.7 billion and that a further commitment of US$2 billion could be reached in 2002, particularly reflecting some large new arrangements, p. 46. The size of individual financing packages has also significantly increased in recent years, both for the regular use of Fund resources as well as for the PRGF, pp. 46-47.

(ii) Need to improve cooperation, collaboration and consensus decision making

A further set of arguments for improved relative voting share and a stronger board presence focuses on the claim of developing countries that there has been a steady decline in the application of key principles which have been used in the past for the conduct of work in the IMF board. Since its inception, the board has generally sought to conduct its work in a cooperative, collaborative manner both among the diverse membership and of course among the Executive Directors themselves.[12]

In this context, it is often said that the board seeks to arrive at decisions based on a broad consensus of the membership. This is certainly the intent of all Executive Directors, who recognise the benefits not only of a congenial and collegial approach to the day-to-day conduct of board work, but who also recognise the value of decision making based on the broadest support among the membership. However, in the context of the claim of developing countries that their voice and representation in the IMF Executive Board warrants strengthening, it is important to understand how the effort to build consensus is achieved in practice.

There is no precise definition of consensus. Optimally, consensus comprises a unanimous decision by all Executive Directors. Many board decisions are indeed taken on this basis. However, in instances where there are important differences of view among the membership, for example between debtor and creditor interests, some departure from a unanimous decision can and often does occur. How then is this latter form of consensus arrived at? As Van Houtven notes, Rule C-10 of the IMF's Rules and Regulations prescribes that the Chair shall 'ordinarily determine the sense of the meeting, in lieu of a formal vote', with the 'sense of the meeting' representing the position supported by Executive Directors who would have sufficient votes to carry the question if a vote were taken. On this basis, the Chair will seek to obtain the broadest spectrum of support, in terms of numbers of Executive Directors and voting share, provided that if put to a vote, there would be more than 50 per cent of the total voting share in favour of the decision. On this basis, consensus could broadly be said to have been achieved when a reasonable majority of the board members, with a reasonable majority of the voting share, agree to a particular decision. It is clear therefore that a consensus would not be considered to have been reached if there were a clear majority of Executive Directors in favour of a particular decision, but the combined voting power of these members was less than half of the total voting power of the board.

On this basis, a consensus which on balance favours the interests of developing countries is very difficult indeed to achieve in the IMF Executive Board.[13] Alliances need to be made with a number of additional Directors from outside the developing country group. To attain even a simple majority of the

[12] See Van Houtven (2002) for an extensive treatment of the efforts which are made to achieve this outcome.

[13] Note that consensus does not mean favouring no group at all, but rather finding a formulation on a particular issue or a particular decision which takes on board the broadest possible spectrum of interests among the members. The outcome of such a process could be consensus-based, yet favour a particular segment or set of interests among the membership.

voting power, the ten Executive Directors representing developing countries would then need to assemble, aside from additional Directors in support of their position, and aside from the combined votes of all eleven Executive Directors representing developing countries, at least a further 20 per cent of the voting power, drawn from members not representing developing countries. In practice this means attracting the support of at least seven non G-7 colleagues, at least six of whom chair constituencies in which creditors hold a majority of the voting power. Based on the current distribution of voting power and of board seats, building a consensus which on balance is in the interests of developing countries is therefore a formidable and near impossible challenge.

Furthermore, what happens if no consensus, based on a broad majority of Directors and a broad majority of the voting strength, emerges? If positions differ, as they inevitably do given the wide range of issues under discussion at any one time, often on detail and occasionally on principle, a basis for arriving at a decision must be used. In practice, for the bulk of day-to-day policy and programme decisions, that basis is decision making based on a simple majority of the voting strength of members. In these instances, simple majority decision making supersedes consensus-based decision making as the deciding factor. With a combined 29 per cent of the voting strength, developing countries face a significantly greater challenge in mobilising a simple majority than the industrial country members, particularly the advanced industrial countries. As can be seen from Table 1.1, where no consensus can be reached and it becomes necessary to secure a simple majority of the voting power, this can quickly be achieved by a collective agreement among the G-7 chairs and a few other directors.[14]

Unless changes are agreed to the overall voting arrangements among members, consensus based decision making in the IMF Executive Board will remain a lop-sided form of consensus, with declining credibility.[15] Consensus in practice means developing countries almost always have to join a consensus initiated and built by the developed country creditors and almost never by developing country debtors. This is despite the fact that most decisions are made in respect of developing country policies and programmes.

---

[14] As can be seen from Table 1.1, a collective agreement between the G-7 members, who hold 47 per cent of the total voting power and any one of five other creditor constituencies, can quickly mobilise a 50 per cent simple majority. Hence, when consensus cannot be reached, it is possible, given the current distribution of voting share, for eight Executive Directors to obtain a decision, when up to 16 Executive Directors are opposed to that decision. In practice, this would be an extreme outcome, which would rarely occur. But it is illustrative of the extent to which weighted voting has now eroded meaningful opportunities for consensus-building. Developing countries argue that the extent of these imbalances are clearly not conducive to collaborative, consensus-based decision making.

[15] Many important decisions require special voting majorities. Van Houtven (2002) notes that there are 40 categories of decisions which require a special majority of voting power in the Executive Board. Of these, 16 require an 85 per cent voting majority and most of the remaining categories, which pertain to decisions regarding financing and operational issues, require a 70 per cent voting majority.

(iii) Institutional inefficiency arising from lack of ownership

In practice, because decisions are always seen to be arrived at based at best on a consensus centred on the interests of creditor members, there has been a growing loss of ownership by the developing countries of board policies. This loss of ownership has been costly to the IMF as a whole and to individual members. It has left scope for poor decisions and inefficient decision making, often based primarily on creditor vs. debtor interests – decisions which are not necessarily in the overall interests of the membership. There is adequate evidence to demonstrate how significantly the imbalance in representation arrangements has affected the efficiency of decision making in the long term. These are most vividly illustrated during periods of crisis. For example, during the Asian crisis in 1997-98, a host of commentators, including several Asian member countries themselves, argued that Fund programme design was inappropriate and failed to take account of specific circumstances of member countries. The quality of decision making and in turn programme design and content would have been far improved and the prospects of success strengthened had the recipient members had a stronger influence in the decision making process. Similar arguments and similar criticisms are noted below in respect of the PRSP initiative.

Similar arguments have also been advanced in regard to the IMF's policy on conditionality. In the past, IMF conditionality has been the subject of extensive criticism. It has been an issue affecting all developing countries with IMF programmes. Despite clear and mounting evidence over many years that programme conditionality had become excessive, irrelevant and counter-productive to the interests of the programmes themselves, decisions approved by the Executive Board continued, over several years, to favour excessive conditionality in IMF-supported programmes. This was despite repeated and well-argued objections by the debtor countries in the board, both to the IMF's policy on conditionality and to the manner in which it was being implemented. Developing countries argue that the lack of voting power to carry their view resulted in substantive failure of the IMF's conditionality policy, caused unnecessary damage to the institution's reputation, and contributed to programme failure in many cases. Fortunately, a fundamental change in conditionality policy was finally agreed, after an extensive consultative process, though only after many years of growing policy failure.[16]

The loss of ownership in policy making is most acutely borne by the IMF's lowest-income developing country member countries. These members, who are eligible for the IMF's Poverty Reduction and Growth Facility (PRGF)

---

[16] Objections to the severity of IMF conditionality have been widespread and persistent. More recently, given clear evidence of the failure of conditionality policy, a new approach to conditionality has been agreed by the IMF Executive Board. The new approach attaches value to parsimony of conditionality and the need for the IMF to focus on conditionalities relevant to its core areas of expertise. The new approach has begun to restore credibility to IMF conditionality policy, though only after over a decade of mounting failure in conditionality policy and immeasurable harm to the institution's reputation. The cost of poor conditionality policy to member countries cannot easily be measured but is considered to have been significant.

programmes, are able to muster barely 6 per cent of the voting power in the IMF board.[17] They have little scope to influence policy and must rely significantly on the persuasive power of their representatives in the board and on the consensus-based style of decision making. As we note below in the case of the Sub-Saharan African members of the board, this makes it all the more important for these members to enjoy an adequate presence, in terms of numbers of seats, in the Executive Board. Their minimal voting strength means that they have no prospect of building a simple majority of the voting power, to generate a decision explicitly in their favour.

There is a similar set of arguments in regard to the PRSP and HIPC processes. For example, lowest-income developing country members raised significant objections, on grounds of both procedure and practice, when the PRSP initiative was launched in December 1999. These included the lack of institutional capacity in their countries to incorporate the new PRSP process and the consequent need for longer timeframes for implementation, the need for PRSPs to be conducted over a period longer than three years, the need for stronger support in linking PRSP objectives to the budget process in member countries, and the need for countries emerging from conflict to be provided with other means to develop poverty-reducing strategies which would nevertheless enable them to qualify for HIPC debt relief at an earlier stage. Although some objections were incorporated at the inception of the PRSP, the bulk of these were overridden because of the overwhelmingly superior voting power of the creditor group. The consequence was that in almost all instances, the PRSP process encountered precisely the challenges and difficulties which developing countries and particularly the PRGF members had predicted. Some of these were corrected during an important review of the PRSP process in 2002, based again on evidence in the field of mounting and valid objections to aspects of the process. But developing countries note that these objections had been raised three years earlier. The three-year delay unnecessarily damaged the institution's reputation as an agency seriously interested in poverty alleviation and resulted in significant and unnecessary capacity constraints on low-income country members. This group of the membership continues to object to some aspects of the design of PRGF programmes. Given the current distribution of voting power and particularly of board representation, these members consider that there is little prospect of redress by relying on their direct experience of the flaws in PRGF programme design, because of their limited voice at the table.

The growing sense of lack of collective ownership of decisions has had another secondary, but serious, consequence for institutional efficiency, by eroding the likelihood of success of individual country programmes. It has meant that in some – fortunately limited – cases recalcitrant policy makers have had a handy excuse for not committing themselves to sound policies, ever aware that they can lay all fault at the Fund's door because programme and policy decisions are perceived to be decided by the creditor members of the IMF.

---

[17] See Evans and Finnemore (2001), who illustrate the fact that HIPC members hold 2.29 per cent of voting share and the remaining non-HIPC PRGF members hold only a further 3.67 per cent.

Additional Concerns of Specific Groups of Developing Countries

As noted above, in their representation arrangements in the IMF Executive Board, developing countries share a host of common challenges and common grounds for claiming improved voice in the board. While there remains a strong degree of homogeneity of interests among developing countries, there is also a range of specific reasons which particular sub-groups among developing countries advance in favour of strengthened voice. For analytical purposes, it is useful to identify at least three significant strands within the developing country group in the IMF board. These include the large emerging market economies, which generally enjoy access to international capital markets, the transition economies and the low-income members, broadly comprising members eligible for the IMF's concessional Poverty Reduction and Growth Facility (PRGF).

Each of these sub-groups among developing countries emphasises specific reasons for improving their voice:

- The large emerging market economies emphasise their claim on the grounds that they are large and growing users of the IMF's resources and that in some cases their economies have grown very significantly in recent years. Their relative quota and hence their relative voting share does not reflect this. These members focus their claims on the methodology used to calculate members' quotas and hence their relative voting strength. They argue that important changes are required in the methods used to determine calculated quotas, to reflect their growing global economic influence. These include changing the basis, in the quota formulae, for converting GDP measured in domestic currency, from a market-based exchange rate method, to the use of a purchasing power parity (PPP) index.[18] In addition, they challenge the weights used in several of the variables included in the quota formulae. Some members also assert that their actual quotas are well below their calculated quotas. Even without a change in the calculation methodology, based on the existing rules for calculating quotas, their actual quotas should be adjusted upward to more closely approximate their calculated quotas, thereby improving their relative voting share.

---

[18] These members note that PPP is used for calculations in the IMF's World Economic Outlook assessments and in other international reports. Moreover, market exchange rates do not necessarily equalise the price of tradable goods across countries, even after allowances are made for quality and transport costs; and they note that the depreciation of market exchange rates may erode or underestimate the GDP growth of some countries in relation to others. The issue of choice of mechanism to convert domestic currency GDP was extensively considered in 2000, in a report of a panel of experts to the Executive Board. Refer to IMF (2000): Quota Formula Review Group, Report to the IMF Executive Board, 2000, IMF, Washington DC.

- A similar case is made by the transition economies, who also argue that the IMF has increased its attention and focus on this category of countries in recent years. Some transition economies also emphasise the fact that they represent a growing claim on the use of Fund resources, as is the case with the emerging market economies.
- The low-income developing country members assert that their share in total voting power and their presence in the board should be improved for several reasons: they represent by far the largest proportion of countries who are members of the IMF; they argue that the principles of collaborative, multilateral and cooperative behaviour on which the institution is supposed to operate are not being adequately upheld given their current minimal voting share and board presence; that poverty reduction has become an increasingly important and indeed a central objective of the institution; and that the approach to determining quotas is inappropriate. This group of developing countries shares some of the arguments of the emerging market economies and the transition economies regarding the relative emphasis which should be placed among the variables used in the quota formulae. But they tend to go further, to suggest that the selection of the variables themselves should be changed to reflect factors which more closely recognise the institutions' focus on poverty reduction. This group accordingly emphasises the need to include a poverty index in the quota formulae. Representing as they do the group on which the IMF focuses a significant portion of both its operational resources and staff time for the purpose of contributing to global poverty alleviation, this group asserts that it deserves a strengthened voting share and an improved level of representation in the board.

Accounting for the Low Aggregate Voting Power of Developing Countries

If the combination of the above three concerns common to all developing countries – the increased role of the IMF in developing countries; a departure from collaborative, participatory and consensus-based decision making; and declining long-term efficiency of the decision making process – as well as the specific range of concerns of the various sub-groups among developing countries, are sound arguments for increasing the collective voting share and board presence of developing countries, why is it that this has not occurred?

- Firstly, successive quota reviews have tended to include a significant equi-proportionate element, or have resulted in a decision not to increase quotas at all. This has resulted in considerable stickiness in adjustments to relative quotas and therefore to relative voting power.
- Secondly, there has been no recognition of the arguments of developing countries, who assert that variables such as a PPP-based method for calculating GDP, as well as indices which include factors such as population and depth of poverty, should be included in the formulae. This

latter set of arguments is particularly applicable to the low-income developing countries, which can identify no elements of the current quota calculation methodology which offer them any hope of an improvement in their relative quota share and hence voting power.

- Thirdly, the relative importance of the basic vote has declined over time, from 11.3 per cent of the total vote, to 2.1 per cent of the total vote at present.[19] This has resulted in developing countries, which represent the largest number of countries in the IMF, losing voting share to the creditor members.
- Fourthly, regarding increasing the number of developing country board seats, there has been no increase in the number of board seats for over a decade. This is despite the fact that there has been a very significant expansion in the membership of the IMF. The decision not to expand the size of the Executive Board is often justified on the grounds that an increase in the size of the board will generate inefficiency. Indeed, quite the opposite effect may result from a modest increase in board size. At the establishment of the IMF, the original 45 member states were represented by a 12-member Executive Board. By 2003, the membership since the founding of the institution has increased by 139 members. At present, the current 184 members are now represented by a board of only 24 Executive Directors. Hence only 12 new board seats have been created, to accommodate 139 new members.[20]

Is there a Way Forward?

Creditor members clearly hold a clear majority of the voting power in the IMF board. Two questions arise from this basic fact. Firstly, should creditors continue to hold a majority of the voting power? And if so, how large should the size of this voting majority be? In providing financing to its members, the Fund operates on principles akin to a credit union. Until such financing arrangements are changed, for an institution which relies significantly on the funding provided by its creditor members, the presence of a majority of voting power among creditors, particularly in respect of decisions which require financing, can be argued to be logical and appropriate. Without an assured majority, creditors would inevitably leave the

---

[19] The implications of the systematic decline in the relative contribution of the basic vote in total voting power are extensively treated in Buira (2002). Buira highlights, inter alia, the fact that a restoration of the relative share of the basic vote in total voting share would significantly increase the voting share of developing countries, while retaining a creditor majority and preserving the US veto. Note also the comparative analysis provided by Buira, highlighting the fact that other international institutions have adjusted the level of their basic votes to preserve the general principle of equality of states, while others have enshrined this principle in their founding rules.

[20] For a more detailed treatment of the impact on Executive Board workload of the comparatively small increase in Board size, see Bradlow (2001). See also Van Houtven (2002), who notes that since the Second Amendment of the Articles of Agreement in 1978, which specified a Board of 20 Executive Directors, the size of the Board has increased by four Directors, while 57 more countries have joined the IMF.

institution and the financing which underpins a major aspect of the institution's work would disappear. On this argument, at least in regard to financing decisions, creditors should hold a majority of the voting power.

Turning to the second question – how large should this majority be, or alternately, to what extent can the creditor-debtor gap in relative voting share be narrowed? The response to this question hinges on a number of factors: firstly on the extent of political will among creditors to adjust downwards the aggregate creditor voting share; secondly on the question of whether all creditors or only a sub-set of creditors would experience a downward adjustment; thirdly, if the former, whether any adjustment would be shared equally among all creditors – either equally in absolute terms or equally based on existing relative share; fourthly, if only a sub-set of creditors were to lose voting share, which would these be and why; fifthly, the influence of all of the above factors on the ability of the US to preserve its current veto on decisions requiring an 85 per cent majority decision of the board; and sixthly, the extent of impact of these decisions on the aggregate European voting share.

While these are difficult questions to answer, applying the collective minds of the IMF membership could generate important progress on some, if not all of these matters. Options and proposals which seek to address these challenges in a manner which takes account of the concerns of both creditors and debtors, while nevertheless achieving an improved voting share for developing countries, are considered in part five of this chapter.

The Special Case of Sub-Saharan African Representation in the IMF Executive Board

Sub-Saharan African (SSA) members' voice and representation capacity are stymied by the effect of two issues: (i) the minimal voting share of SSA members in the IMF Executive Board; and (ii) the number of board seats afforded to members from SSA.[21] SSA members argue that these factors have resulted in their marginalization from the decision making processes of the institution. They argue that both of these factors can be corrected with minimal adjustment to the interests of the overall membership, but with significant benefits. Benefits would accrue to the institution as a whole, in terms of improved efficiency through better quality of decision making in regard to policies for poverty reduction, a recovery of credibility regarding the consensus-based approach to decision making and a significant restoration of the concept of uniformity of treatment among members.

There are currently 45 SSA member countries in the IMF. This represents almost exactly a quarter of the institution's 184 members. Of these SSA members, almost all (44) are represented by two Executive Directors.[22] These two Directors hold a combined voting share of merely 4.4 per cent. Hence nearly 25 per cent of

---

[21] Refer to Memorandum of African Governors to IMF Managing Director, Special Meeting of Africa Group 1 Constituency, Maputo, Mozambique, June 1999.

[22] Note that one SSA member (Ghana) is also represented by the constituency chaired by Iran.

the combined IMF membership have 4.4 per cent of the voting share; and have two of the 24 available board seats. Using any conceivable measure of fairness or efficacy, SSA members argue that this represents an almost irrelevant share of both vote and seats.

The allocations do not resonate with the IMF's objective of addressing the interests of low-income developing countries. SSA's share of voting power has remained consistently low throughout successive quota reviews and in recent reviews has even declined. In the early years of the Fund, this approach might have been explained by the relatively small share of the institution's human resources, time and financial resources allocated to its SSA members and by the fact that there were far fewer SSA members of the institution in earlier decades. But at precisely the time that SSA's quota and hence its relative voting share has declined, the needs of its members and the role of the Fund in SSA have both vastly increased. Unlike the IMF's role in earlier decades, in recent years there has been a growing range of critical policy issues on which the IMF board now regularly decides, which directly affect the interests of SSA members. All of these policies have directly influenced the IMF's work in SSA member countries.[23] These include policy decisions on:

- The HIPC Initiative: Decisions regarding the HIPC Initiative have occupied a considerable portion of the board's time, particularly since 1996. Aside from the regular HIPC progress reviews, there have been important policy decisions in regard to tracking Poverty Reducing Public Expenditure in HIPC member countries (2002), and Debt Sustainability in HIPC member countries (2002). Of the twelve members eligible for HIPC at 30 April 2002, but which had not yet reached the decision point, ten were from SSA.[24]
- On Poverty Reduction Strategy Paper (PRSP) policies and processes: there have been several board discussions focusing on the PRSP, including the extensive deliberations at its launch and a major review of the program in March 2002. The majority of PRSP cases are from SSA. A significant portion of the institution's resources now focuses on assisting members develop sound PRSPs. The IMF has hosted several major international conferences on the PRSP and sought to actively link the PRSP process with the objectives of the Millennium Development Goals.

---

[23] A key impetus to the IMF's involvement in low-income countries occurred in December 1999, when the Executive Boards of the IMF and the World Bank launched the PRSP initiative; and in the same month, the IMF Executive Board transformed the former Extended Structural Adjustment Facility (ESAF) into the PRGF. The two decisions also inter-linked the IMF's role in the HIPC initiative with both the PRSP and the PRGF initiatives. The combination of these two decisions placed poverty reduction at the centre of the IMF's work in low-income countries; and marked the beginning of a significant increase in the institutional resources, as well as Executive Board time, devoted to policies and programs in low-income countries. For a detailed outline of the range of IMF initiatives to help reduce poverty, refer to Chapter 5, IMF Annual Report, 2002.

[24] Refer to Table 5.1, IMF Annual Report, 2002, p. 53.

- On the Poverty Reduction and Growth Facility (PRGF): almost all SSA members are now pursuing PRGF programmes. Aside from the extensive involvement of the board during the process of transforming the ESAF into the PRGF there has been a significant review of the PRGF in March 2002.

SSA experience looms large in board discussions of conditionality, domestic ownership of Fund programs, on support to countries emerging from conflict, and on the Fund's policies in regard to arrears.

The Growing IMF Role in Low-income Countries: Implications for Workload of SSA Constituencies

Aside from the increase in policy work for low-income countries, SSA members also draw attention to the direct increase in workload in the SSA constituencies, resulting from the IMF's increased role in poverty reduction. SSA members in the Executive Board argue that an improvement in both their voting share and the number of board seats made available to their members is warranted on the grounds that a very substantial share of the IMF's work on poverty reduction now focuses on SSA. These members point to the fact that SSA is now the focus of:

- the overwhelming bulk of the IMF's work on the Heavily Indebted Poor Country (HIPC) debt relief initiative;[25]
- a very large share of the IMF's PRGF programmes;
- the large majority of its work on Post-Conflict Assistance;[26]
- and almost all of the IMF's protracted arrears cases.[27]

In addition, these members note that SSA represents the largest user, in comparison with any other region, of PRGF resources.[28] SSA members also observe that in recent years they have become increasingly reliant on the IMF as one of their few remaining significant sources of international financial assistance. For member countries so reliant on the resources of the institution, it is therefore inappropriate that they should have so negligible an influence on the policies which directly affect their interests.

---

[25] Of 27 HIPC countries to which the IMF had committed resources as at 30 April 2002, no less than 23 were from SSA. Refer to Table 6.3, IMF Annual Report, 2002, p. 62.

[26] On 30 April 2002, four of the six members receiving the IMF's concessional post-conflict emergency financing were from SSA. Refer to Table 6.2., IMF Annual Report, 2002, p. 63.

[27] Of seven IMF member countries in protracted arrears to the IMF at 30 April 2002, five were from SSA. These members had combined protracted arrears of SDR2.298 billion, representing 97.6 per cent of total protracted arrears to the IMF. Refer to Table 6.7, IMF Annual Report, 2002, p. 69.

[28] The extent of IMF focus on Africa is highlighted by the fact that by the end of April 2002, over two dozen SSA members were preparing PRSPs with IMF assistance; and 23 members had qualified for HIPC debt relief.

Consequences of Declining Relative Voting Share of SSA Members

With an improved voice for SSA members, board efficiency and effectiveness in regard particularly to the IMF's work in low-income countries could have been far more effective. The absence of adequate voice has meant a direct and unnecessary cost to the Fund's reputation and its ability to succeed in its own objectives of reducing poverty, by not adequately understanding and incorporating the views of a significant share of the membership, on a set of issues which in fact affects a majority of the IMF's member countries and on which these countries have the most incisive and direct experience and knowledge. Clearly more voices speaking on behalf of SSA would offer a greater opportunity for representatives of the region to articulate the needs of SSA members and much greater scope to forge a consensus on many of the matters of crucial interest to these members.

SSA members contend that the PRSP framework, for example, was established during a key board meeting in December 1999, ignoring many of the concerns of the low-income countries and many of the key objections raised by SSA members.[29] Both the World Bank and the IMF Executive Boards corrected some of the defects identified by low-income countries in the PRSP process, but only three years later and amid clear signs that the approach contained significant defects.[30] The weighted voting structure had muted the voice of those members that knew most about the issue, resulting in deficiencies in the PRSP and unnecessary damage to the reputation of the institution and hence to all its members.

The second important consequence of the combination of minimum voting power and minimum board presence has been to generate an impossibility-of-performance scenario. The two SSA Executive Directors have at least double the number of PGRF countries in comparison with any other non-SSA constituency. In addition, most member countries within the two SSA constituencies are also HIPC-eligible, adding considerably to the workload. Furthermore, all of the remaining IMF arrears cases are now within the SSA fold.

---

[29] Concerns pertained to the process through which the PRSP would be initiated, rather than the principle of a country developing a poverty reduction strategy. Relevant and legitimate issues were raised regarding the pacing and phasing of PRSPs, the need for different approaches to PRSP preparation, the lack of domestic capacity to prepare PRSPs in many countries, the lack of fiscal resources to give effect to the recommendations which PRSPs were likely to generate; diversion of policy-maker's efforts from other crucial activities, including their macroeconomic reform efforts and their efforts to secure bilateral and multilateral debt relief. Only a few of these objections were translated into amendments to the framework at inception.

[30] Refer to Public Information Notice (PIN) No. 02/31 – IMF Executive Board Reviews the Poverty Reduction Strategy Paper (PRSP) Approach, which reviewed progress with the PRSP. Many issues on which progress was made during this review were issues which had been raised three years earlier by SSA and other low-income country members when the PRSP was conceptualised.

The third and very significant adverse consequence of the low voting share/low board presence combination has been to erode – and with the growth of SSA membership in the Fund, to effectively remove – any realistic possibility that these members can build a consensus. For the SSA members consensus decision making has come to mean joining a consensus already built by other members. Consensus building is immeasurably easier if seven or eight members of the board hail from the same region and decide to join forces on a particular issue or on a particular policy. To achieve a reasonable measure of consensus in the board, these members would need to persuade not much more than four or five Executive Directors of their view and, if they comprise the largest creditors and if consensus were to be put beyond challenge, they would need few if any additional votes to achieve a simple majority. If the two large SSA members, notwithstanding that they represent a quarter of the members of the institution, decided to join forces equipped with 4.4 per cent of the vote, they would need to find at least ten other supporters in the board and at least 45 per cent of the vote, to build a consensus.[31]

A fourth consequence of the absence of effective representation for SSA members has been to contribute to progressively reducing member programme ownership, thereby undermining domestic commitment to reform.

Several commentators have begun to recognise the extraordinary situation of the SSA members in the IMF Executive Board. The most detailed presentation of this issue thus far is that of Evans and Finnemore (2001), who after a detailed assessment assert that 'the obvious remedy would be to divide the two African constituencies in half and add two more African EDs'. As the authors note, this would not necessarily require changing voting shares, and under certain circumstances might also not require increasing the size of the board.[32] The issue of inadequate representation of SSA board members has also been noted inter alia by Bradlow (2001) and Mohammed (2002). Within the IMF itself, there has been some recognition that the representation of SSA members has become an important challenge.[33] In addition, a number of further papers have suggested considering a change in the rules, to enable any constituency with a specified number of members to elect an Executive Director; or setting a ceiling on the number of member countries represented by any one chair.[34]

---

[31] It is hardly surprising that for these board members, the incentive to actively build consensus is muted and viewed as something of a Herculean and effectively Don Quixotic challenge.

[32] Refer to Evans and Finnemore (2001), pp. 13-14.

[33] See Van Houtven (2002), who notes that 'The low voting strength of the two sub-Saharan constituencies, which together amount to 4.4 per cent, is among the issues of concern in the size and structure of the Board in view of the exceptionally large number of member countries in the sub-Saharan groups, 45, many of whom have policy programs with the IMF and need technical assistance as well', p. 22.

[34] See for example Alberich and Martinez (2002). The authors make a strong appeal for open and transparent rules for the election and appointment of Executive Directors.

Options for Improving Representation of Developing Countries in the IMF Executive Board

This section considers some potential options for reform of both the voting structure and the distribution of Executive Board seats in the IMF, which would address the substantive concerns of developing countries in the board, and significantly address the challenges of loss of ownership of the decision making process and attendant loss of efficiency in decision making.

Several types of options are suggested: first, all-inclusive dialogue among shareholders, and second, options which seek to address the imbalance in voting power. These include proposals based on a pre-determined creditor-debtor voting structure and those focusing on specific sub-groups among developing countries. Third, there are options addressing the size of the board. Finally, additional proposals and options for improving developing country voice in the Executive Board.

There are no simple options. The suggested options are in most instances not mutually exclusive. All options would require broad political consensus among the membership. Because of the zero-sum nature of aggregate voting power, most options, though not all, necessarily imply that there would be some losers and some winners. Similarly, in addressing the imbalance in representation based on the current distribution of board seats, most scenarios imply that there are likely to be some winners and some losers.

A. *Dialogue*

Option 1: Establish a committee of the Executive Board
Directors could examine the key issues and report to the Board of Governors. The report could be either an extensive treatment of the issue, containing recommendations, or it could constitute a brief statement of the key aspects of the challenge. The advantage of this approach would be that it would include the views of Executive Board members themselves, thereby providing a direct overview of the day-to-day challenges experienced by Directors. A disadvantage could be that the issue could prove to be too contentious to address at the level of the Executive Board, placing unnecessary strain on the regular conduct of board operations.

Option 2: Establish a committee of the Board of Governors
To initiate a broad shareholder dialogue, the Board of Governors could establish a committee representative of the membership, to examine the issue and to report back to the Board of Governors. The advantage of this approach would be that the discussion would be mandated at the highest level and would avoid a potentially disruptive process from emerging in the Executive Board.

Option 3: External review
An external agency could initiate a process of dialogue among a broad cross-section of the membership, to identify the key aspects of the challenge of developing country representation, to seek consensus and to identify areas in which progress may be able to be made; and to make recommendations to advance the

issue. The advantage of this approach would be that a dialogue could begin relatively promptly. A disadvantage would be that the process would not have been initiated by a wide cross-section of the IMF's membership.

B. Adjustment of Voting Shares

Option 4: An agreement on raising voting share

There could be an understanding that the voting share of developing countries, or more precisely of IMF debtor countries, would be established at some percentage below 50 per cent, but considerably more than the current level. Decisions on how this increase was to be allocated within the developing country group could be left to developing countries. Decisions as to how the corresponding decrease would be effected from among the developed countries would be taken at the time of the in-principle decision of the amount of reallocation. It could be agreed to phase the implementation of such a decision over a medium-term cycle of 2-3 quota review periods, thereby minimising potential for sudden and large corrections.

What is feasible in terms of reallocation? At present, creditor members hold a very significant majority of the voting power. As noted earlier, their voting share by country is 61.5 per cent; and by virtue of the current distribution of Executive Board seats, creditors are able to increase their voting power to 70 per cent. It would be reasonable to propose a downward revision in overall creditor share which resulted in creditors in the IMF holding a voting majority, of approximately 52 per cent. This would result in an approximately 10 per cent reallocation of voting power to debtor members. The retention of a permanent creditor majority in the IMF could be structured to preserve the US veto and could also be structured to retain a significant European voting share, including the current European veto. In addition, depending on the mechanisms used to effect such a revision, the relative ranking of voting strength among the creditor group could be preserved, either entirely or to a large extent.

If political agreement were unable to be achieved to improve the interests of all developing country members, a further set of options would be to agree to enable one or more sub-sets within the debtor group to benefit from an overall political agreement to improve their voting status. These options include:

Option 5: Increase the basic vote

A similar option would be to increase the basic vote by an agreed margin.[35] This option would have the advantage of being applicable to all members of the institution, would not result in any reduction in voting share of any members, and would correct the significant decline in the voting share of the smallest members of the IMF. Many authors have proposed restoring the basic vote to its relative share in the total vote at the time of establishment of the IMF, hence increasing the share of the basic vote in total voting share from 2.1 per cent to 11.3 per cent. The precise degree of adjustment would require a political consensus among the membership. As Buira (2002) shows, increasing the basic vote to its relative share

---

[35] Many commentators have recommended this option. See for example Buira (2002).

of the total vote at the time of inception of the IMF would preserve the US veto, maintain an overall European member veto and maintain a creditor majority in the total vote. It would also increase the share of developing country vote to approximately 47 per cent, thereby considerably narrowing the creditor-debtor gap, while still maintaining a creditor majority.

Option 6: Return the basic vote to original level of significance
The weakness of Option 5 is that the relative influence of the larger developing countries – typically the emerging market economies – would decline despite the fact that they represent the largest users, in quantum of resources, of IMF resources. A variant on the Option 5 would be to agree to increase the basic vote by a specified percentage – perhaps some level less than the 11.3 per cent needed to restore the level set at the IMF's establishment; and to combine this with a selective allocation to some developing countries. The combined effect of the increase in basic vote and the selective increase to specified developing countries could be pre-determined, resulting, for example, in a net increase in developing country voting power equivalent to that which would occur had the basic vote been restored to its level in 1944, or to any level agreed by the membership as a whole.[36] This approach could also be used to address the concerns of some Asian members, that the influence of Asian members in the global economy has grown and merits an increase in relative quota and shareholding.[37]

Option 7: Migrate to a PPP approach
To address the strong preference among emerging market economies, transition economies and many low-income countries that a PPP-based method of computing GDP is a more appropriate approach than the current exchange rate-based approach, there could be a gradual migration from the current approach to the PPP method. The migration to a PPP approach could be agreed to take place in steps, over for example two or three 5-yearly quota reviews. This would entail a gradual shift over a 10-15 year period, thereby allaying the fears of some members that their voting share would be significantly adversely affected. An envisaged final timeframe, for example 2018 or 2023 (15 or 20 years hence) could be agreed, by which time a final approach would be expected to be fully implemented. This option could also include the concept of a floor on the downward adjustment of

---

[36] The determination as to which developing countries would benefit from the selective portion of such an increase would depend on the objectives. Groups of members who could justifiably benefit include the emerging market economies, some transition economies and the stronger performers among the PRGF countries. A selective increase could also be used to achieve certain political objectives which might be perceived to be in the interests of the overall membership, including facilitating some members, for example SSA, from exercising a leadership role within this group, in the IMF board. At present, the presence of two SSA board seats, each with over twenty members, results in the inability of even the largest members within each group from exercising leadership on behalf of the group. This situation would be further accentuated in any scenario increasing the basic vote.

[37] The suggestion that an increase in basic vote would need to be re-balanced by some selective increases to emerging market members is taken up in Buira (2002).

voting share of members most significantly prejudiced by the change, in each round of correction and on aggregate. In this manner, the adjustment would not precipitate a sudden pronounced correction in relative voting shares. However it would, over time, correct a significant flaw in the methodology used for computing GDP. The approach could also serve as an incentive for those countries which have not yet developed a PPP-based measure of GDP, to do so within a reasonable timeframe. For countries which currently do not have PPP-based data, the average degree of correction among all other member countries could be applied, or some other basis mutually agreed by the collective membership, in computing their quota share.

Option 8: Focus on income PRGF-eligible members
There could be an agreement to increase the collective voting share of the low-income PRGF-eligible members by a specified percentage; and deducting such share from all other members. The deduction could be achieved in several ways: by deducting a fixed number of votes from each non-PRGF member; by effecting deductions based on existing relative shareholding with the larger shareholders relinquishing a comparatively larger proportion of their voting share; or some other commonly agreed method. Depending on what method was used to reallocate voting power, an advantage of this approach could be that in relative terms, all non-PRGF members could retain their relative ranking in voting terms, while the PRGF members would increase their aggregate voting share. Furthermore, because the relative share of PRGF members in total voting share is minimal, their relative shareholding could be significantly improved – for example doubled or tripled – without a significant adjustment in the voting shares of the non-PRGF members. This option would enable the IMF to give substance to the claim that it is willing to hear the views of its clients; and would significantly promote ownership of its policies and programmes, by the institution's members. Note that in preference to 'deducting' votes from some members, the same outcome could be achieved by allocating a selective quota increase to the PRGF members.

Option 9: Focus on SSA members
To address the low aggregate voting share of SSA members, this option would consist of a political agreement among the combined membership to: (a) ensure that the combined voting share of SSA members does not decline beyond its current level; and (b) to allocate the SSA members a predefined share of the total voting power. This share would be greater than the current level of 4.4 per cent, with any increase being drawn from an agreed pool of non-SSA members. Since the overall aggregate increase would be likely to be relatively small, perhaps an adjustment of between three to four per cent, spread among a large segment of the membership and possibly among all non-SSA members, the adverse implications for each non-SSA member would be negligible. In addition, the current relative ranking of voting share among the non-SSA members could be maintained, by an agreement to this effect by all members. The net effect of this option would be to preserve the relative voting ranking among all non-SSA members, while increasing SSA's share in the total vote. This would allow for several benefits. Firstly, it would address the acute imbalance which has developed in SSA's overall voting

share. Secondly, it could be structured to permit the creation of a third and possibly fourth SSA Executive Board seat, each with a meaningful voting share (see Option 10 below). Thirdly, it could be structured to benefit SSA members selectively rather than collectively, for example favouring those members who have been high performers within the group, those who can offer strong leadership to the group and those for whom a special case is warranted.

C. *Size of the Board*

Option 10: Add board seats

Establish one or two additional board seats for SSA members. The advantage of this approach would be to eliminate the impossibility of performance which has in the past characterised SSA board representation; to allocate the work load among three or four rather than two constituencies; and to enable SSA members to achieve effective representation in the IMF board. Note that a sub-division of the existing two seats into three seats, with approximately 15 members per seat, would result in the three SSA members continuing to have the largest workloads among all 26 board members of a reconstituted and enlarged board.[38]

A method of achieving the same outcome, without explicitly favouring any specific region, would be to set a ceiling which is represented by an Executive Director. If the ceiling on the number of countries were set at ten members per constituency, this would result in three more seats for SSA members, and would also require some non-SSA constituencies that represent more than ten members relinquishing some members. In practice, a ceiling of 13-15 members would constitute an optimal outcome, ensuring that SSA members secured at least one additional board seat, and enabling all other constituencies to remain intact, or to effect a voluntary reshuffling if they considered it desirable.

An ancillary challenge presented by this approach would be determining how the resulting three African constituencies would be comprised. Some reshuffling within the current two constituencies would clearly be required. In practice, this challenge would be addressed internally among Sub-Saharan African countries. There are optimistic grounds that a suitable arrangement could be established, as a number of key entities could be utilised to help forge a broad Sub-Saharan African agreement on the composition of the three African chairs. These could include the African Union, the NEPAD, as well as contributions to this determination by key regional institutions in East, West and Southern Africa.

It is often suggested that the circumstances of SSA members can be adequately addressed by assigning these members an additional Alternate Executive Director position and/or by increasing the number of staff in the Executive Directors' offices. Implementing these suggestions would certainly

---

[38] Even with one additional board seat, SSA members represented by three constituencies would continue to have the largest number of PRGF program countries, members with PRSPs, HIPC members, members emerging from conflict and members in arrears to the Fund. In practice, however, the current impossibility of performance engendered by a two-seat SSA representation in the board would be ameliorated.

ameliorate one aspect of the challenge confronting SSA members: the impossibility of adequate performance given the large number of member countries represented in each of the two current constituencies, the large number of programme, off-track, post-conflict and arrears cases within them, as well as the challenge of representing a very large share of HIPC members. In this regard, a recent decision by the Executive Boards of both the IMF and the World Bank, to allocate three additional Advisor (IMF) and Senior Advisor (World Bank) positions to the constituency offices represents a significant step forward in helping ameliorate the workload in the two offices. The increase in staffing to the SSA constituency offices, although an important improvement, is unable to address the work in large intensive constituencies of more than twenty countries, each with more than 17 programmes that are either active or in intensive-care mode. It is unable to address the challenge of diminished member country ownership in the decision making process itself, nor the challenge of enabling SSA members to have meaningful opportunities to forge and join a Board consensus.

To increase the board's size (an 85 per cent majority is required), it is often argued that an increase in size will contribute to decreased operational efficiency. It should be noted, however, that any such decrease, were it to occur, would be marginal, given the addition of up to two more seats to the current 24. Any losses in efficiency would be likely to be far more than compensated for by the benefits.

As regards the prospect of a decrease in the size of the board, to enable one or two more SSA seats to be created, this would clearly require an extraordinary political consensus among the collective membership. In practice, as many commentators have noted, this would most likely be achieved by reducing the number of European chairs in the IMF board, from the current 7-8, to (if only SSA claims to further board seats were to be considered) 5-6 seats.[39] In this regard, the possibility of a union between the French and German seats has been considered; and a further possibility could be to achieve agreement among the remaining 5-6 European chairs, to a reduction in one further European seat. In practice, unless there is agreement to enlarge the size of the Executive Board, which appears unlikely given objections by the large industrial countries and particularly the USA, the resolution of the current acute minimisation of Africa's voice in the IMF Executive Board will only be able to be resolved once the European chairs determine how to reduce their representation, including the number of European board seats, in the IMF Executive Board.

---

[39] There are strong grounds for proposing a reduction in the number of Directors representing European members: the region already has by far the largest number of seats in the Board in comparison with other regions, while its GNP is only 70 per cent larger than that of the US which has a single chair; in addition, increased regional integration in Europe has rendered the region more akin to a single monetary, economic and trading bloc, suggesting the possibility of reducing the number of board seats to a single seat. This of course would be a radical change in representation arrangements and on balance would not be in the interests of the collective membership of the IMF. However, some reduction from the current 7-8 seats would be reasonable. For a discussion of some options for reducing the number of European seats as well as the aggregate European vote, see, for example, Buira (2002).

Option 11: An additional Asian seat

An additional board seat would reflect the increased economic strength of Asian member countries. It would be perceived to address an imbalance, by recognising the growing influence of Asian members in the world economy. In practice, the creation of such a seat would be likely to favour Korea, whose economic growth has been particularly pronounced in recent years. Per the provisions of the Second Amendment of the Articles of Agreement, this option would also require an 85 per cent voting majority of the Board of Governors. An important disadvantage of this approach is that it would tilt the overall balance among the (non-SSA) developing countries away from the current perceived approximate balance between Latin America, Asia and the Middle East, toward a stronger representation by Asian members.[40] For this reason, it is often argued that the preferred approach to recognising the increased influence of Asian economies is to increase the relative quota of selected Asian members, on the basis suggested in Option 6 above.

D. Further Options and Proposals

Option 12: A further detailed set of options has been suggested by Kelkar et al. (2003)

These options, which would also require broad political consensus, involve separating the various functions served by quotas. Kelkar *et al.* note that the basic problem of the quota formulas has been a classic assignment problem, namely a mismatch between the number of instruments and objectives. Currently, there is only one instrument, namely the quota that is aimed at achieving multiple policy objectives such as determination of members' contribution to the Fund, their access to Fund resources and their influence in the governance of the Fund through voting rights. Kelkar *et al.* suggest that the number of instruments should be not less than the number of policy objectives. As there are three policy objectives, at least three instruments are needed. To achieve this, quotas should be confined principally to determining members' contributions to Fund resources; quotas should be delinked from policy and a greater role should be assigned to the Westphalian principle (one country one vote) in the determination of voting rights. The proposals of Kelkar *et al.* would represent a very significant departure from current practice.

Option 13: Increase ED terms and staff

This option would address the challenge of lack of institutional memory and staffing constraints of the developing country members. The length of service of all elected Executive Directors could be increased to between three and five years. This would enable developing country Executive Directors to acquire greater influence, through the ability to become more familiar with Fund policies and

[40] At present, Latin American and Caribbean members have three seats (headed by Brazil, Argentina/Chile and Mexico/Venezuela, the latter except in two of every six years, when Spain assumes the chair); Asian members, excluding Japan, have three seats (China, India, and Thailand/Indonesia) and one alternate position (Korea); and Middle Eastern members have three seats (Egypt, Iran and Saudi Arabia).

practices, as well as board procedures. Regarding staffing constraints, one option would be to allocate additional staff on the basis of the number of member countries in a constituency with IMF-supported programmes. A specific proposal would be to allocate an additional Advisor position for every three member countries supported by IMF programmes. As the number of member countries with IMF-supported programmes in a given constituency would vary over time, some historical averaging could be used to determine the additional staff numbers to be assigned per constituency. Coupled with the existing policy of allocating staff on the basis of number of countries represented, the advantage of this approach would be that it recognised the varying degrees of intensity of workload.

Conclusion

Creditors in the IMF Executive Board should, particularly in regard to financing decisions, maintain an assured majority of the voting power. But as this chapter has argued, the current margin beyond that required to assure a simple majority has become illogical and excessive. Collectively, the excess surplus of votes held by the creditor group beyond a simply majority of votes strikes at the foundation of the principles of collaboration and consensus decision making upon which the Fund operates, weakens the institution, reduces operational efficiency, gnaws away at the institution's legitimacy, erodes ownership of programmes and policies by the collective membership, has bred understandable resentment by the debtor group and offers no tangible benefit to the collective membership. In recent years the excess majority of voting power has also precipitated a range of efforts by the more powerful debtor members to find other institutions and mechanisms to express their opinions. All of these arguments suggest that a narrowing of the extent to which creditors hold a voting majority in the IMF board would be desirable and in the collective interests of the membership as a whole.

While the size of the Executive Board has evolved over time to take account of the growth of the membership, some important inconsistencies have developed in this process – in particular the disproportionate number of constituencies representing European members; and the fact that accommodation for growth in membership has been made for all but the two large Sub-Saharan African constituencies. Correcting the second inconsistency need not have a bearing on the first challenge, but requires a decision to increase the size of the board.

Some innovative new proposals have been suggested which re-examine the multiple functions of IMF quotas. Detailed examination of these could yield options for progress in correcting the imbalance which has developed in regard to developing countries' voice in the IMF Executive Board. It would be useful to actively find methods to discuss these proposals.

The terms of duty of Executive Directors should be lengthened, to improve the capacity of developing country Executive Directors to contribute to policy and programme discussions and to build institutional memory in their constituencies; and staffing rules would benefit from reforms which took account of relative intensity of workload. While intensity is difficult to define, one useful proxy is the number of countries in a constituency with IMF-supported programmes. Supplementing the existing rules which assign staff based on number of countries represented with this approach, would help alleviate the disproportionate burden on developing country constituencies.

All potential options require political consensus among the membership and the preservation of the factors to which creditors attach significant importance, including the principle of creditor majority, the US and European veto power and relative ranking among creditors. Mechanisms should be found to initiate consideration of these options.

References

Alberich I. and M. Martinez (2002) *Quotas and Representation in the International Monetary Fund*, International Department, Bank of Spain.

Bradlow, Daniel (2001) 'Stuffing New Wine into Old Bottles: The Troubling Case of the IMF', *Journal of International Banking Regulation*, **3**(1).

Buira, Ariel (2002) *A New Voting Structure for the IMF*, The Intergovernmental Group of Twenty-Four, Washington DC.

Buira, Ariel (2003a) *An Analysis of IMF Conditionality* (paper prepared for the XVI Technical Group Meeting of the G-24, Port of Spain), United Nations, New York.

Buira, Ariel (2003b) *Reforming the Governance of the Bretton Woods Institutions in Financing for Development* (proceedings of a Workshop of the G-24), published by The OPEC Fund for International Development.

Evans, Peter and Martha Finnemore (2001) *Organizational Reform and the Expansion of the South's Voice at the Fund*, G24 Discussion Paper No. 15, Washington DC.

IMF (1944) Articles of Agreement, Washington DC.

IMF (1995-2002) Annual Reports, Washington DC.

IMF (2000) *Quota Formula Review Group*, Report to the IMF Executive Board, 2000, IMF, Washington DC.

IMF (2001a) *Financial Organization and Operations of the IMF*, Washington DC.

IMF (2001b) *IMF Executive Board Discusses Conditionality*, Public Information Notice (PIN) No. 01/28, March, Washington DC.

IMF (2001c) *Strengthening IMF/World Bank Collaboration on Country Programs and Conditionality*, Public Information Notice (PIN) No. 01/92, September, Washington DC.

IMF (2001d) *IMF Reviews Strengthening Country Ownership of IMF-Supported Programs*, Public Information Notice (PIN) No. 01/125, November, Washington DC.

IMF (2002a) Annual Report, Washington DC.

IMF (2002b) *IMF Executive Board Reviews the Poverty Reduction Strategy Paper (PRSP) Approach*, Public Information Notice (PIN) No. 02/31, IMF, Washington DC.

IMF (2002c) *News Brief 02/63: Guidance on Design and Implementation of Conditionality*, 11 July 2002, IMF, Washington DC.

IMF (2002d) *New Conditionality Guidelines*, IMF News Release No. 02/42, September, Washington DC.

IMF (2003) *IMF Board Recommends to Governors Conclusion of Quota Review*, Press Release No. 03/02, IMF, Washington DC.

Kapur, Devesh and Richard Webb (2000) *Governance-related Conditionalities of the International Financial Institutions*, G-24 Discussion Paper No. 6.

Kelkar, *et al.* (2003) *Reforming the Governance of the International Monetary Fund* (forthcoming).

Meltzer Commission (2000) *Report of the International Financial Institution Advisory Commission*.

Mohammed, Aziz Ali (2001) *The Future Role of the IMF*, G24 Discussion Series Paper No. 11, Washington DC.

Mohammed, Aziz Ali (2003) *Burden Sharing at the IMF*, Paper prepared for the XVI Technical Group Meeting of the G-24, Port of Spain.

ODC Task Force Report (2000) *The Future Role of the IMF in Development*.

Quota Formula Review Group (2000) Report to the IMF Executive Board, IMF, Washington DC.

Van Houtven, L. (2002) *Governance of the IMF: Decision Making, Institutional Oversight, Transparency and Accountability*, IMF Pamphlet Series, Washington DC.

Wood, A. (2001) *Structural Adjustment for the IMF: Options for Reforming the Governance Structures*, Bretton Woods Project, London.

Woods, N. (1998) *Governance in International Organisations: The Case for Reform in the Bretton Woods Institutions*, International Financial and Monetary Issues, Research Papers for the G24, United Nations.

Woods, Ngaire (2000) 'The Challenge of Good Governance for the IMF and the World Bank Themselves', *World Development*, **28**(5).

Woods, Ngaire (2001) 'Making the IMF and the World Bank More Accountable', *International Affairs*, **77**(1), January.

Chapter 2

Democratizing the IMF

Andrew Eggers, Ann Florini and Ngaire Woods[1]

Introduction

Calls for the IMF to democratize abound. The demands for greater participation in IMF decision making are coming from many sources, including non-governmental organizations, trade unions, religious groups, and grass-roots groups. They have a compelling case. First, like any organization working closely to meet and further the needs of its clients, the IMF needs constant feedback from its member countries and peoples affected by its programs in order to keep up the quality and relevance of its own policies and decisions. Second, IMF lending and conditionality typically takes place during a crisis when the IMF and finance ministry officials of a country must make decisions without time to engage in broad democratic consultations. If the Fund's role is not to be coercive, then the participation of the broader society must precede the crisis and be part of the normal politics of engagement between a country and the IMF. Finally, globalization and its detractors have intensified scrutiny of all international organizations and the IMF, like all others, must demonstrate and reinforce its claim legitimately to set standards and influence economic policies in its member countries.

Despite the clear need to democratize the Fund, little rigorous thought has been given to how to make that happen. Obviously democracy in this context does not mean holding popular elections for Fund officials. Instead, the question is how to allow citizens affected by Fund operations and policies to exercise accountability over the relevant decision makers and to have voice in the decisions.

There is no single answer, no one mechanism that will magically resolve the dilemmas of global democracy. But there are several steps that would constitute real progress. One would be to find meaningful ways to increase the involvement of parliamentarians, who in most countries are intended to be the

---

[1] Andrew Eggers is Senior Research Analyst at the Brookings Institution. Ann Florini is Senior Fellow at the Brookings Institution and author of the recent book *The Coming Democracy: New Rules for Running a New World*. Ngaire Woods is Director of the Global Economic Governance program at University College, Oxford and author of a forthcoming book on the politics of the IMF and the World Bank. The authors wish to thank Chas Budnick for valuable research assistance, and many senior staff members and country representatives at the IMF for their useful comments and suggestions on an earlier draft of this chapter.

channel through which citizens have voice in national decisions. In a few, mostly rich, countries, legislators already weigh in on IMF issues, but most parliamentarians do not. In this chapter, we describe and evaluate the status of parliamentary involvement to date, and recommend how both parliamentarians and the IMF itself can bring about more and better parliamentary oversight.

A Changing Institution

Democratic process was not a priority when the IMF was first established. At the time, the rules governing international organizations were those of diplomacy, not democracy. Protecting the confidentiality of negotiations took precedence over direct accountability to citizens. The IMF had a mission of monitoring the pegged exchange rate system. This seemed to require oversight only by the most technically qualified components of national governments, the Treasury/finance departments and central banks. Thus, it seemed logical to have general oversight provided by a Board of Governors consisting of such officials (usually the finance minister or the head of the central bank) from member governments. Day-to-day direction of the Fund's activities was, and is, provided by Executive Directors who report to (and usually are selected by) the finance ministry or central bank of the relevant member(s).[2] The Articles of Agreement provide that 'each member shall deal with the Fund only through its Treasury, central bank, stabilization fund, or other similar fiscal agency, and the Fund shall deal only with or through the same agencies'.[3]

Since the collapse of the pegged exchange rate system in the early 1970s and the debt crisis in the 1980s, the Fund's activities have changed beyond recognition. It has evolved into a key provider of development assistance. For many countries it is now also the ultimate arbiter of whether international capital will be made available at all. The Fund's use of conditionality has hugely expanded. These changes have led to a storm of objections about the Fund's perceived usurpation of the prerogatives of sovereign governments.

---

[2] The IMF website describes the role of the Board of Governors as follows: The *Board of Governors*, the highest decision making body of the IMF, consists of one governor and one alternate governor for each member country. The governor is appointed by the member country and is usually the minister of finance or the governor of the central bank. All powers of the IMF are vested in the Board of Governors. The Board of Governors may delegate to the Executive Board all except certain reserved powers. The Board of Governors normally meets once a year.

It describes Executive Directors as follows: The Executive Board (the Board) is responsible for conducting the day-to-day business of the IMF. It is composed of 24 Directors, who are appointed or elected by member countries or by groups of countries, and the Managing Director, who serves as its Chairman. The Board usually meets several times each week. It carries out its work largely on the basis of papers prepared by IMF management and staff.

[3] Article V (1).

In 2001, in response to growing criticism of the intrusiveness and political infeasibility of many of its loan conditions, the IMF began revising its overarching philosophy on loan conditionality. New conditionality guidelines were heralded as a way to signal the institution's intention to reduce the scope and depth of the IMF's involvement in fundamentally political matters. Subsequently, operational guidelines have amplified how this new philosophy should be put into practice.[4] The new approach entrenches four principles that ideally ought to guide Fund officials' approach to conditionality: (1) ownership, meaning that the IMF must interact in ways which permit countries to take the lead, and that Fund officials must continue talking and not walk away from negotiations; (2) parsimony of goals; (3) focus on conditions which clearly lead to specified goals; and (4) clarity as to what is and what is not a condition of the loan. It bears noting that the actual implementation of these new guidelines will require serious and active monitoring and enforcement not just by senior management within the Fund but also by its Executive Board – indeed, the not-so-different previous conditionality guidelines were honoured more in breach.

These revisions, while welcome, will not by themselves resolve the democratic deficit in the IMF. The Fund remains deeply involved in political matters. In effect, as the IMF's role has changed it has become part legislature, deciding or strongly influencing what policies countries will adopt and how they will spend funds, part executive branch, heavily influencing how those policies will be implemented, and part agency of restraint on governments, holding them to explicit targets and policy objectives and monitoring their performance in achieving these goals. Yet the Fund's governance structure has not changed to reflect its new roles.

The Democracy Gap

At best, there is a tenuous link from the IMF to citizens it affects. In a handful of rich-country democracies, citizens elect politicians, some of whom form a government that appoints ministers who appoint an Executive Director, who usually need not report to anyone other than the minister. Some rich countries share Executive Directors, but the largest shareholders each have their own and can replace him or her at any time – holding him or her directly to account for his or her actions on the board. Contrast this to the lack of accountability of Executive Directors to the developing countries, all of whom are grouped in constituencies represented by one member of the board who cannot be replaced at the whim of any one government. Consider a person living in an undemocratic country with no opportunity to elect (or throw out) his or her government. The unelected government joins with other governments, sometimes similarly unelected, to select, in a closed-door process, a single Executive Director who must represent all the countries in that constituency.

[4] www.imf.org/External/np/pdr/cond/2003/eng/050803.htm.

Other chapters in this volume address the issue of whether the IMF's governance structure should undergo fundamental reform that would require renegotiation of the Articles of Agreement to change the relative voting power of rich and poor IMF members. This chapter examines a more immediately applicable set of reforms: how might citizens in all countries better hold the IMF to account and exercise voice in its decisions, much as they would expect to do with their own governments, within the existing structure and rules of the organization?

This chapter focuses particularly on the role of parliamentarians as potentially the key and most legitimate interlocutors between societies and governments. It describes a situation very much in flux, with parliamentarians, non-governmental activists, and IMF staff and Executive Directors already grappling with difficult questions about how best to ensure adequate accountability and voice. It assesses the existing role of parliamentarians in holding the board accountable and in shaping Fund policies and programs. It concludes with recommendations for enhancing that role.

Underscoring the analysis is the assumption, now openly recognised by the IMF, that the institution's effectiveness depends upon a greater engagement with parliaments and citizens within countries. Compliance with Fund-supported policies, even where they are narrowed to a focused minimum of conditionality, cannot be achieved simply by enhancing the Fund's public relations. Key groups within countries must be drawn into the process of formulating, monitoring and implementing policies. In the current jargon, 'local ownership' of policies is critical if the IMF's work is to be successful. But this must go beyond consultations as currently conducted by the Fund.

Why Focus on Parliaments?

To date parliamentarians have played relatively little part in oversight of the IMF. An array of non-governmental advocacy and campaigning organizations has attempted to fill the gap. Spurred on by the growing influence of the IMF on developing countries in the 1980s and 1990s, particularly the impact of structural adjustment programs, many groups came together to attempt to influence the IMF directly. They have campaigned on a wide range of issues, from labour rights to environment to corruption. The largest efforts have centred on poverty, debt relief, and the processes of decision making at the Fund. The range of tactics reflects the range of groups and issues: everything from street protests at the Fund's annual meetings to correspondence and meetings with senior staff and Executive Directors to engagement with member governments and parliaments.[5]

---

[5] For a detailed account of the role of civil society groups at the IMF, see Robert O'Brien, Anne Marie Goetz, Jan Aart Scholte, and Marc Williams, 'The International Monetary Fund and Social Movements', in *Contesting Global Governance: Multilateral Economic Institutions and Global Social Movements*, Cambridge, Cambridge University Press, 2000, pp. 159-205.

There is no question that the efforts of NGOs have borne fruit. Thanks in substantial part to their demands, the Fund is a far more transparent and less secretive organization than it was a decade ago, and it pays at least some attention to some of the substantive issues raised by the campaigners. However, with a few notable exceptions, non-governmental organizations lack the sustained funding and expertise needed for concerted campaigns on Fund issues.

Moreover, relying on civil society groups to serve as the channel for public voice into the IMF is problematic. Which voices to include or exclude is often decided haphazardly, or relies upon the Fund itself to act as a gatekeeper, picking and choosing with whom it will consult.[6] Inevitably the best-funded, largest, and best-located NGOs end up with disproportionate attention. This magnifies the voice of Northern citizens within the Fund since they have more chance to influence both their powerful government representatives in the institution as well as their home-grown NGOs and their parliaments.

More philosophically, non-governmental organizations may lack the legitimacy that accrues to members of parliaments when those members are elected. In democracies, parliamentarians channel and balance the sometimes competing interests of various elements of civil society. In exercising this role, they are held to account not only by elections but by each other through parliamentary rules and processes, by their political parties, and by counter-balancing institutions of government including the courts, ombudsmen and such like. Non-governmental organizations are not always held to account. They need to attract members and funding and hence they need media attention and public support; but few are subject to any form of representative or democratic accountability.

At the local level, the use of non-governmental organizations as the sole way to link citizens to the IMF risks eroding efforts to strengthen democracy and accountable government by sidestepping local representative institutions such as parliaments, particularly in developing countries. This risk is heightened by the Fund's new propensity to consult at local levels with non-governmental groups in efforts to broaden support for agreements it forges directly with executive branch agencies.

This is not to argue against the right of such groups to engage the Fund and its member governments however they (peacefully) can. Such public engagement is a crucial element of good governance, whether at the national or global level. But it cannot be the sole mechanism for channelling citizen voices.

Fortunately, the engagement of civil society can actually strengthen the incentives and possibilities for parliaments to hold the Fund to account. Their monitoring and publicizing of the IMF's activities has served to draw attention to the IMF and not least to generate parliamentary interest in and scrutiny of the IMF, especially in Northern legislatures.

---

[6] The Fund has now published a guide to assist staff in conducting outreach which outlines how they might build positive relationships and how such outreach might assist them. The guide can be accessed at www.imf.org/external/np/cso/eng/2003/101003.htm.

Overseeing the IMF in Northern Parliaments

Parliaments in the larger creditor countries of the Fund have always had at least nominal power to oversee the Fund's business. As holders of the power of the purse, their assent is necessary before the IMF can increase its financial resources. Further, using their powers to review, question, and legislate ministry of finance policy, they can technically exert oversight and control over the actions of the government's Executive Director on the IMF board.[7] In practice, parliaments for most of the life of the Fund have not taken up active oversight roles. But in recent years, as the Fund's purview has broadened and its activities have become increasingly controversial, parliaments in a number of creditor countries in the North have become more active with regard to the Fund. They have summoned, questioned, and grilled officials from their ministry of finance and the IMF itself. They have rejected or threatened to reject IMF quota increases, and made approval contingent on specific IMF reforms. They have passed legislative mandates requiring Executive Directors to pursue certain policies at the Executive Board.

While many national legislatures are capable of exerting influence on IMF governance and many legislatures have increasingly done so, the US Congress has taken a far more active oversight role than any parliament. Accordingly, our review of the record of legislative oversight of the IMF is largely devoted to evaluating and analyzing the Congressional experience. The role of Congress is important not just because Congress has been responsible for the bulk of legislative oversight but because its forays into Fund governance suggest some of the possibilities and pitfalls of further expanding parliamentary oversight of the IMF. But while the example of Congress provides some useful lessons for legislators around the world who seek to increase their oversight role, one of the key conclusions to be drawn from observing Congress's experience with the IMF is that no other parliament is likely to produce the kind of oversight, positive and otherwise, held by Congress. Advocates of parliamentary oversight have expressed the hope that, if other legislatures would simply follow the example of Congress, Fund governance would become much more democratic. Others have cautioned that Congress's oversight has been politicized and misguided, and the Fund would be damaged by more such activism. A close look at the history of Congressional oversight and emerging efforts in other legislatures suggests that both these hopes and fears are overdrawn.

The Singular Case of the US Congress

Why has the US Congress been the torchbearer of legislative oversight? Since the US has the largest share of votes on the IMF board (and veto power on crucial matters such as quota increases), Congress clearly has a larger incentive to become

[7] The power of parliaments to legislate international financial policy varies, of course, from political system to political system. Further, this power is significantly smaller in countries that share an Executive Director among other countries in a constituency and in cases where the ED reports to an independent central bank rather than the finance ministry.

involved in IMF matters than do other legislative bodies. Located on the other side of Washington from the IMF's headquarters and blessed with generous staff and funding resources, Congress also has fewer logistical obstacles to realizing that influence than do other legislatures. But the overwhelming reason for Congress's extraordinary role is that the US political system provides Congress with extraordinary powers over the US executive branch. The US has a system in which the president can be, and often is, from a different political party from the one that controls Congress. Congress's most significant Fund oversight efforts have taken place at moments (such as 1983 and 1998) when Congress and the White House were at odds in ways that are impossible in the parliamentary systems of the other major creditors.

Congress's oversight of the IMF is characterised by long periods of neglect punctuated by brief flurries of activity. Treasury provides Congress with regular reports about IMF business and committees in the House and Senate attempt to stay apprised of Fund developments, but international financial issues ordinarily occupy such a low place on the political agenda that IMF business generally receives very little attention. On a number of occasions in the past several decades, though, political forces and economic events have converged to put the Fund at the centre of legislative controversy. By examining two of those episodes, in 1983 and 1998, we hope to illuminate the circumstances that make Congress the most active legislative overseer of the IMF. It should be clear that Congressional oversight has often been driven more by narrow domestic politics than by the challenges of global economic governance. It should also be apparent that Congress is an extraordinary case, and that no other legislature can be expected to play as dynamic an oversight role on IMF matters. Still, Congress's experience highlights some of possibilities and limitations of using domestic legislatures to democratize decision making at the Fund.

Two Episodes of Focused Congressional Attention

In 1983, the IMF proposed a US$33 billion increase in IMF quotas and an US$18.5 billion increase in the General Agreements to Borrow, which amounted to a roughly 50 per cent increase in the IMF's total resources. This dramatic expansion came on the tail end of the Latin American debt crisis that began in Mexico in 1982. The Fund set a deadline of 30 November 1983, for member country approvals, and the Reagan administration put its support behind fulfilling the US commitment. According to US law, expanding the quota requires Congressional authorization, so the Republican administration called on a split Congress (Democratically-controlled House of Representatives and Republican Senate) to act.

A fight ensued in the US Congress, which touched on issues of legitimate concern (such as moral hazard in international bailouts), but in the end hinged on narrow domestic political agendas. Democratic leaders in Congress made their support of the proposal contingent on the administration's approval of a measure that would increase subsidies to provide low-income housing. Meanwhile, Republican lawmakers pushed for language requiring the US to oppose IMF measures in communist countries. Two privately-organized right-wing anti-

IMF campaigns used radio advertisements and mailings to claim that the IMF was turning Uncle Sam into 'Uncle Sucker', financier of delinquent borrowers and communist dictators in unsavoury regimes in Iraq, Laos, Tanzania, and Mozambique.[8]

A combined IMF-housing bill finally passed Congress on 18 November 1983. Along with subsidies for low-income housing, it included compromises on the substance of US policy at the IMF. Instead of requiring the US Executive Director to automatically oppose loans to communist countries and to South Africa, as critics had initially insisted, the final bill required the Treasury Secretary to explain any favourable US vote on such loans and, if requested, appear before Congress to justify the vote.[9] The legislation also included mandates requiring the US Executive Director to pursue a set of policies designed to reduce moral hazard in IMF lending, increase transparency, and promote free trade.[10]

An even more dramatic collision between the IMF and Congress took place in 1998, when the IMF, recently stung by the Asian Financial Crisis of 1997, proposed a 45 per cent quota increase. The Democratic Clinton Administration asked a Republican-led Congress to approve the jump in the US contribution. In the ensuing debate, opponents used politically popular isolationist themes but also expressed broader concerns including: the moral hazard problems inherent in bailing out bankrupt regimes; qualms about the IMF's excessive political influence in post-crisis Asia; outrage that the IMF had provided loans to ruthless regimes like Suharto's government in Indonesia without opposition from the US representative; and (from Democrats) misgivings about the insufficient emphasis on social safety net programs and labour standards in the IMF's reform programs.

In the end, dissatisfaction with the IMF coalesced around the issue of transparency. In the legislation passed in October 1998 that finally approved the quota increase, Congress imposed a new set of mandates requiring the US ED (Executive Director) to take on a broad reform agenda at the IMF addressing transparency, exchange rate stability, sound banking principles, good lending, and a dozen other priorities. Treasury was also required to make more frequent and thorough reports to Congress, including updates on the progress of Congress's proposed reforms. Most importantly, Congress created a commission chaired by Professor Allan Meltzer (who had been on record arguing that the IMF should be abolished[11]) to investigate the functioning of the IMF and other international financial institutions and propose reforms. The Meltzer Commission reported back in 2000 with a sharply critical series of proposals designed to limit the scope of

---

[8] Leonard Silk, 'The Campaign Against IMF', *The New York Times*, 19 October 1983, D2.

[9] Hobart Rowen, 'Massive IMF, Housing Compromise is Approved by Senate, 67 to 30; Major Changes Seen in Lending', *The Washington Post*, 18 November 1983, D8.

[10] U.S.C. 286z-gg, 30 November 1983. See GAO Report GA 03-401R, 'Treasury Maintains a Formal Process to Advance U.S. Policies at the International Monetary Fund', February 2003.

[11] Allan Meltzer, 'Why it is Time to Close Down the IMF', *Financial Times*, 16 June 1995, p. 21.

IMF activity and make the Fund more accountable to national governments (especially the US government).

While these are only two episodes in the story of Congress's oversight of the IMF, the dominant features of these episodes are typical of Congress's role in Fund governance. One key point is that Congress was moved to act by a quota increase proposal which it had the authority to approve or reject. (And since an IMF quota increase cannot take place with the approval of members with 85 per cent of quotas, Congress has effective veto power over the entire proposal.) The bulk of Congressional activism towards the IMF has occurred at times when quota increases have been under consideration. The political stakes of these approval processes are somewhat heightened by 'sticker-shock'. The 1998 quota increase, for example, came to US$17 billion, and although raising the quota by US$17 billion costs the US far less than US$17 billion, this point was usually lost in the course of Congressional debates.[12]

Another important point is that these battles took place when Congress and the White House were controlled by different political parties. Opposing the quota increase provides Congress with a way of expending the President's political capital and exacting concessions on unrelated partisan issues, as was the case with housing for the Democratic House of Representatives in 1983. Less cynically, constraining the US ED with legislative mandates offers a means for Congress to impose its partisan policies on the executive branch.

Another central factor is that in both 1983 and 1998 the IMF had recently gone through a highly-publicized and criticized financial crisis – the Latin American debt crisis in 1982 and the Asian Financial Crisis in 1997. These episodes elevated the importance of international finance as a public policy issue and led to public pressure, particularly channelled through NGOs, in favour of changing the Fund's course.

Types of Congressional Oversight

Congressional oversight of the IMF can be separated into two types: review and control. Review is the most basic and, in the end, the most essential form of legislative oversight of the IMF. The US Congress currently requires a number of reports from the Treasury Department, including a quarterly report on the US Executive Director's votes on new programs and semi-annual reports on foreign exchange issues, which ordinarily involves IMF policy discussion. As an outgrowth of the Meltzer Commission process, Treasury must file annual reports on its efforts to promote US policies at the Fund and on governance reforms taking place at the Fund, such as increasing the transparency or changing the extent of

[12] Interview with Jon Rosenwasser, former professional staff member to the U.S. Senate Budget Committee responsible for international affairs, March, 2004. Although Treasury argues that there is actually no cost to an IMF quota increase (since it is an exchange of monetary assets rather than an expenditure), there is a cost from interest rate risk and valuation adjustments. Thus the true cost is somewhere between zero and the 'sticker price'.

IMF conditionality requirements.[13] Congress has also relied on its research agency, the General Accounting Office (which has a US$432 million annual budget and a 3200 person staff)[14] to conduct ten major studies of IMF policies since 1998 (and one each in the 1970s and 1980s).[15]

On occasion, Congress has engaged in IMF review through fact-finding projects of its own. For example, in April of 1998 a House Banking subcommittee called on United States Executive Director Karin Lissakers to testify. Along with another Treasury official, Lissakers underwent nearly two hours of hostile questioning, in which legislators asserted that, in the recent IMF bailout in Indonesia, the US ED's office had neglected Congress's instructions to oppose IMF programs in countries with records of human rights abuses.[16] Members of Congress and their staff have also attended annual meetings of the IMF, although since they attended as visitors they did not have access to policy making meetings or even have much opportunity to question senior staff.

In contrast to oversight through review, oversight through control consists of attempts to dictate IMF policy. One way in which Congress has exercised control has been to make the release of approved funding conditional upon particular IMF reforms. For example, Congress replied to a 1994 IMF request for US$100 million for an Enhanced Structural Adjustment Facility (ESAF) program by providing US$75 million and promising the rest when a list of confidential IMF documents, including policy framework papers, were made public.[17] This condition led to an important step forward in IMF transparency. Again in 1998, the US Congress made its approval of the major quota increase conditional on several reforms designed to improve accountability and reduce high-risk investment. For its part, the IMF has generally satisfied the US conditions, but not without claiming that these were reforms that the IMF was already working on anyway, and that no single country would force reforms on the Fund.[18]

As we have already indicated, another way in which Congress has exercised control in IMF matters is through legislative mandates dictating the policies that the US ED must pursue on the board. As of 2003, there were 67 such

---

[13] The Treasury Department is required to provide semi-annual foreign exchange reports to Congress under section 3005 of the Omnibus Trade and Competitiveness Act of 1988. Reporting about the progress of US policies at the Fund is pursuant to Sections 1503 and 1705 (a) of the International Financial Institutions Act and the Consolidated Appropriations Act for Fiscal Year 2000, P.L. 106-113 section 504(e), cited in GAO-03-401R, 'Treasury Maintains a Formal Process to Advance US Policies at the International Monetary Fund', p. 1.

[14] The United States General Accounting Office, 'GAO at a Glance', www.gao.gov/about/gglance.html.

[15] These studies are available on the GAO's website, www.gao.gov, by searching for 'International Monetary Fund', in the 'Title' field of the site's search page.

[16] David E. Sanger, 'IMF Loans to Rights Violators Are Attacked in Congress', *The New York Times*, 22 April 1998.

[17] Pratap Chatterjee, 'Accountancy: Uncertain Returns from a 50-year Investment – Why the IMF and World Bank are Coming under Greater Scrutiny from their Backers', *Financial Times*, 21 July 1994, p. 14.

[18] 'Congress Approves $18 Billion for IMF', 22 October 1998.

legislative mandates currently in force prescribing US policies at the Fund, the oldest dating from 1945.[19] Congress's legislative mandates can be divided into two broad categories, policy mandates and directed vote mandates.[20] Policy mandates identify policy priorities of the Congress and direct the US ED to use his 'voice' and/or 'vote' to pursue those priorities. For example, a policy mandate in the 1998 quota increase legislation asks Treasury to instruct the US ED to use his voice and vote to promote policies that will open markets for agricultural commodities and reduce trade barriers.[21] Directed vote mandates more specifically require the US ED to oppose particular types of IMF programs; one such mandate that was passed in 2002 requires the US ED to oppose any loans to the Cambodian government, except to support basic human needs.[22]

What is the effect of these mandates on IMF policy? The answer depends on both the content of the mandate and the standards by which we measure effectiveness. One way to judge the policy mandates is by the extent to which the mandate succeeds in persuading the IMF staff to consider an issue in designing a program. By this standard, most policy mandates have been ineffective because they address issues that the IMF staff considers distant from the Fund's core macroeconomic focus. Currently active mandates regarding environmental and labour conditions, female genital mutilation, and trafficking in women address important issues, but not concerns the IMF staff typically view as sufficiently relevant to economic stability and growth to be determinants of IMF program policy. (If anything, the staff would argue, these are issues for the World Bank or other multilateral development banks.) On issues such as these, the US ED essentially goes through the motions of advocating Congress's policy by making statements at board meetings and requesting the staff to pursue the matters further; the staff, already occupied by more macroeconomically-relevant issues, generally declines to add the issues to the institution's research agenda. This is especially true for proposals that are not only irrelevant to macroeconomic stability but seem to narrowly promote American interests, such as a 2000 mandate requiring the US ED to promote the use of US clean coal technology in infrastructure programs.[23]

Some policy mandates have no effect because they echo already-accepted IMF policy. For example, a directed vote mandate that emerged from the 1983 quota increase controversy essentially articulates standard financial reasoning about moral hazard and debt rescheduling;[24] a 1978 measure (also prompted by a quota increase) requires the US ED to encourage the IMF staff to formulate economic stabilization programs that foster investment and employment;[25] and a

---

[19] Report of Joseph A. Christoff, Director, International Affairs and Trade (GAO), 'International Monetary Fund', GAO-03-401R, 7 February 2003.

[20] GAO's 2003 report 'Treasury Maintains a Formal Process to Advance US Policies at the International Monetary Fund', GAO-03-401R, employs this distinction.

[21] 22 U.S.C. 262n-3, 21 October 1998.

[22] P.L. 107-115, section 563, 10 January 2002.

[23] P.L. 106-429, section 537, 6 November 2000.

[24] U.S.C. 286dd, 30 November 1983.

[25] 22 U.S.C. 286e-9, 10 October 1978.

1998 mandate encourages the US ED to work to strengthen the financial systems of IMF member countries and promote sound banking principles and practices.[26] In each case, the legislative mandate reflected what was already considered to be the core IMF mission at the time.

It is on issues that reside between these two extremes of irrelevance and redundancy that legislative mandates have the greatest potential to affect IMF policy. Yet it is difficult to find examples of policy mandates to date that fit that description. Perhaps with time and repetition, the US ED's statements in observance of Congress's policy mandates will lead to changes in the IMF's priorities in designing programs. To be sure, none of Congress's more self-serving policy mandates (such as a 2000 mandate requiring the US ED to work toward the maximum use of American goods in IMF programs) will change any minds in the IMF staff. But it may be that persistent efforts to follow up on Congress's mandates on sex trafficking or female genital mutilation, now considered irrelevant to IMF policy, may lead to the IMF staff changing its view of what is relevant.

In the case of directed vote mandates, the issue becomes slightly more complicated. Since the US has the largest single bloc of votes on the Executive Board (17 per cent), its votes can make a difference in deciding IMF policy. Approval of a country's IMF program requires support from a majority of the board so the US cannot unilaterally block access to IMF funds. Still, an excessively self-serving or otherwise inappropriate directed vote mandate from Congress cannot be politely ignored as are many of its policy mandates. At this point, the directed vote mandates generally require the US ED to adopt predictable positions opposing funding of terrorist states, communist dictatorships (a holdover from 1983 quota increase legislation), and specific states (Cambodia, Sudan and Burma). Occasionally, one is nakedly self-serving, as in the 1986 mandate forbidding the US ED from supporting programs that would lead to production for export that would hurt US industry.[27]

Of the total of 26 directed vote mandates, only a few stand out as having a substantial effect on IMF policy. One example is the 1996 mandate requiring the US ED to oppose IMF assistance to countries that do not conduct and report regular audits of their military spending to civilian authorities.[28] Starting in 1999, the US ED was required to vote against or abstain on an IMF program if the program country appeared on a blacklist compiled by a newly-formed US Interagency Policy Group (convened by Treasury and made up of representatives from the Department of State, the Department of Defense, the US Agency for International Development, the National Security Council, and the Office of Management and Budget). As of 2000, 17 countries were on the list (Treasury did not disclose which ones), and the US ED's office had abstained on three programs in the first year the mandate was in effect. The IMF staff is generally supportive of

[26] 22 U.S.C. 262o-2, 21 October 1998. This mandate is examined in depth in GAO-01-214.

[27] 22 U.S.C. 262h, 15 October 1986 (also repeated in P.L. 107-115, section 514, 10 January 2002).

[28] 22 U.S.C. 262k-1, 30 September 1996. Congress passed four separate mandates concerning military audits beginning in 1992.

the idea of military audits, since military spending is clearly a relevant sign of a country's commitment to economic development and a measure of the extent to which IMF funds are being used for the purposes intended. Still, the IMF does not require military audit data as a condition for its programs, so US efforts to identify countries that failed to meet its standards has heightened the visibility and importance of military spending discipline in many cases.[29] One measure of the success of the mandate is that non-compliant countries such as Burkina Faso, Rwanda and Guinea-Bissau have made efforts to get off the list in order to continue receiving aid.[30]

Not surprisingly, Congress has been interested in determining whether its mandates are having the desired effect at the IMF. Part of the controversy in the 1998 quota increase battle in Congress was the extent to which the US ED's office appeared to be flouting Congress's list of mandates. One of the conclusions lawmakers arrived at during the questioning of US Executive Director Karin Lissakers was that the US ED's office was not following up on legislative mandates at the IMF.[31] As a result, in 1999 the US Treasury Department instituted a formal process systematically to promote these policies at the IMF. The process relied upon a special departmental task force to seek out opportunities to advance the mandated policies through dialogue with Fund staff, discussions with program country officials, and formal statements at the Executive Board.[32] As mentioned above, the General Accounting Office is now required to report annually on the extent to which the US ED is working to promote its mandates at the IMF.[33]

Members of the US ED's office have expressed concern that the legislative mandates actually reduce their influence in board discussions.[34] The ED's obligation to rehearse points mandated by Congress lessens the impact of any attempt to add more specific reflections on an issue or program. In the case of directed votes, mandates can also restrain US influence. The fact that everyone knows that the US will vote 'no' on a Cambodia program circumscribes the ED's ability to shape that program. Still, EDs find ways to make their opinions known, even when their statements and votes are governed by Congress, or a Treasury Department for that matter. It is not difficult for the ED to follow the letter of the mandate in board discussions while making clear the independent position of the ED's office.

---

29 GAO-01-214, p. 60.

30 GAO-01-214, pp. 57, 63.

31 David E. Sanger, op. cit., p. A8; Nancy Dunne, 'IMF Chiefs Face a Grilling from a Lone Warrior of Capitol Hill: Bernie Sanders is Taking on the Might of the White House and Most of the Senate', *The Financial Times Limited*, 21 April 1998, p. 6.

32 'International Monetary Fund: Efforts to Advance US Policies at the Fund', GAO-01-214, p. 6.

33 Consolidated Appropriations Act for Fiscal Year 2000, P.L. 106-113 section 504(e), cited in GAO-03-401R, op. cit., p. 1.

34 This point is made in GAO-01-214, pp. 18-19, 71.

Prospects for Legislative Oversight in Other Creditor Countries

Parliaments in other creditor countries generally have the same opportunities to oversee IMF policy that are available to the US Congress. A legislative action is required in each of the major creditor countries before a quota increase can be passed.[35] To varying degrees, parliaments in these countries also have the legal authority to legislate national policy toward the IMF. But no other parliament has the degree of oversight or political controversy on IMF issues approaching what we have seen in Congress. In part, this has to do with the US's special place in the IMF; since no country has anything near the US's voting share (Japan, with 6.15 per cent of the votes, is second to the US's 17.14 per cent[36]), no parliament has as much of an incentive to try to shape IMF policy. But the predominant reason why parliaments have taken a smaller role must be that, in parliamentary systems, the legislature has a less adversarial relationship with its cabinet than Congress does with the US administration. Parliaments and their cabinets are controlled by the same party, so IMF policy making is less likely to become a battle in an intra-governmental partisan war in the way it periodically has in the US Congress. This is an obvious point of comparative politics but it must be remembered as we contemplate the likely effects of a further opening up of the Fund on parliamentary involvement.

Since IMF oversight in legislatures outside of the US occurs in a less politicized environment, other creditor parliaments are extremely unlikely to adopt the same brash and controlling tactics as has the US Congress. Still, in recent years parliaments have increasingly acted as conduits for citizen concerns about the IMF and signs of active oversight have proliferated.[37] Both the UK parliament and the French National Assembly began receiving reports on IMF matters from government in 1999, and others, including Ireland (1999) and Italy (2003), passed their own laws introducing reporting on IMF issues.[38] Special committees in the UK and French legislatures have closely tracked IMF issues and produced thorough and useful reports. The UK House of Commons has also hosted IMF

---

[35] In most cases, a parliament must make an amendment to the legislation through which a nation joined the IMF, such as the 'Bretton Woods and Related Agreements Act' in the case of Canada. In the UK, the 1979 International Monetary Fund Act established that quota increases would be undertaken via statutory instruments, which are orders promulgated by the Treasury, laid before the House of Commons for 14 days, and then approved by a resolution of the House.

[36] 'IMF Executive Directors and Voting Power', updated 29 February 2004. www.imf.org/external/np/sec/memdir/eds.htm. Last checked 31 March 2004.

[37] Our discussion of European parliamentary oversight of the IMF benefited from an internal background paper, 'Parliamentary Scrutiny of IFI Issues in Europe', prepared by Agir Ici, a Paris-based NGO working on global development issues. This research is available from Agir Ici on request.

[38] On UK and France: Tavernier, pp. 205-206, email from Alex Wilks, 13 May 2003. On Ireland: Interview with Carol Welch, Friends of the Earth, 29 April 2003. On Italy: email from Antonio Tricarico of Italian NGO CRBM, 30 March 2003, to Carol Welch *et al.*

Managing Director Horst Kohler for a heated question-and-answer session.[39] Kohler later made appearances before the German Bundestag, the Dutch parliament, and the Chilean Senate, although the IMF is careful to stress that its officials never 'testify' before parliaments, maintaining that IMF staff cannot be called to account in this manner.

Perhaps the most striking recent example of parliamentary activism on IMF matters outside of the US occurred in Italy in March of 2003. The Italian Senate used the occasion of its 1.12 million euro replenishment of the PRGF (Poverty Reduction Growth Facility) to lay down a number of policy prescriptions which, although non-binding, the government accepted as directives. It instructed the treasury to promote better transparency and participation in the PRGF process, to support the adoption of revised parameters for the evaluation of the environmental and social impacts of PRGF processes, and to work for the development of an improved arbitration mechanism within the IMF. Further, the treasury was directed to report on the IMF spring meeting and describe what steps were undertaken to further the above agenda. Most significantly, the PRGF funding was made nominally conditional on the treasury fulfilling these obligations. (Since the directives did not hold the force of law, neither did the conditionality of the funding.[40]) The Senate's muscular treatment of the Italian treasury on IMF issues suggests that parliamentary activism outside the US may more frequently move from review to control.

Still, for the foreseeable future, no parliament other than Congress is likely to burden the Executive Board with mandated pro forma statements or apply serious pressure on its government and the IMF by threatening to reject a quota increase. This point is extremely important because Congress's oversight of the IMF is often mentioned as an example of the dangers of involving national legislatures in Fund governance. In our view, the fundamental differences between the US Congress and other legislatures mean that, even if the Fund follows recommendations to further open its operations to scrutiny, it will not likely face more of the controlling behaviour it has seen from Congress. On the other hand, because other legislatures do not have as adversarial a relationship with their cabinets as is the case in the US, there are limits to the positive contributions that creditor country legislative oversight is likely to make.

The Emerging Involvement of Parliaments in Southern Countries

Parliaments in borrowing countries have typically had very little involvement with the IMF. The terms of an IMF structural adjustment program are usually decided upon in negotiations between the IMF staff and the finance ministry and central bank of the country concerned. Parliamentary approval is critical to the implementation of many of the more extensive Fund programs, since privatization

[39] The transcript of the exchange is available at www.publications.parliament.uk/pa/cm200102/cmselect/cmtreasy/uc868-iii/uc86802.htm.

[40] Emails from Antonio Tricarico of Italian NGO CRBM, 30 March 2003 and 23 March 2004.

programs, fiscal reforms, and financial system restructuring usually require new legislation. That said, the IMF has typically expected borrowing country parliaments to accede to the terms of the agreement, or at least has left the task of winning parliamentary cooperation to its interlocutors in the ministry of finance. A series of rebuffs from program country parliaments and growing parliamentary interest in development policies have forced the Fund to put much more effort into consulting and persuading program country parliaments.

Parliaments played leading roles in two of the most well-publicized recent economic crises: Russia in 1997-1998 and Argentina in 2001-2002. Russia's relationship with the IMF in the late 1990s presented one of many battlefields in the brutal political struggles over market reform that took place between President Yeltsin and a parliament heavily laden with recalcitrant communists. IMF loans to Russia included a number of conditions, each of which provoked political fire fights: tax reforms to increase revenues and rationalize an inconsistent and corruption-prone system; spending cuts on the military and state-subsidized industries; and the break up of nationwide gas and electrical monopolies. Parliament at first ignored and then fought back against these requirements. As Russia's economic crises deepened over the winter of 1997 and spring of 1998, the IMF continued to provide loans despite the government's failure to follow through on loan conditions. In July 1998, a day after a new US$17.1 billion loan agreement was negotiated, parliament flatly rejected a number of the tax reforms that were key conditions of the loan. President Yeltsin vetoed several of the parliament's laws and began to institute required reforms by decree. The IMF, wanting to send a message to lawmakers, reduced the value of the first instalment of its loan. The power struggle between Yeltsin and parliament continued as Russia's currency was devalued and the crisis hit bottom in August of 1998. Even after the IMF reengaged with Russia the following spring, it continued to face sporadic parliamentary resistance to IMF-sponsored reforms.[41]

Argentina, once considered a model program country, defaulted in December 2001 on US$155 billion in foreign debt, the largest default in history. The IMF quickly suspended aid. Argentina requested financial assistance from the Fund in early 2002 and was met with a list of conditions including monetary adjustments, spending cuts, and politically sensitive reforms to the system of revenue-sharing with the provinces. Seeing no choice, the government met most of the IMF's demands, but the parliament was more stubborn, refusing to move on a bill converting savings to bonds while flouting IMF orders by passing bills reforming bankruptcy rules and punishing 'economic subversion' which removed money from the cash-strapped economy. Legislators faced stiff pressure from the IMF and the government to step into line, but also confronted burgeoning popular resistance to

[41] This account is based largely on a series of articles written by Michael R. Gordon in the *New York Times* during the crisis 'Pressures for Change Mounting in Russia', 2 January 1997, p. 13; 'Russia Reaches IMF Accord to Free Loans', 13 December 1997, p. 1; 'Russia Resists IMF's Strategy for Reducing Budget Deficit', p. 3, 16 May 1998; 'Russia and Lenders Seal Accord on $17 Billion in New Support', p. 1; 14 July 1998; 'Parliament in Russia Fails to Pass Bills Tied to Loans', 18 July 1998, p. 4.

IMF-led reform, including demonstrations in which bank account holders and other protestors surrounded the Senate and refused to let legislators enter.[42] With the IMF and parliament still at loggerheads over the 'economic subversion' statute, Argentina sank further and threatened to default on loan payments to the World Bank unless it obtained more assistance from the IMF. Ultimately, the IMF provided a 'transitional loan' of US$6.78 billion, forestalling further crisis but leaving unresolved major disagreements between parliament and the Fund.

In several less well-known cases, national parliaments have refused to abide by the terms of agreements in which they had no voice. In Turkey in 1998, parliament forced the government to break its promise to the IMF to hold down the wage increases of public sector workers.[43] In 1999 and 2000, the Moldovan parliament repeatedly rejected IMF-mandated privatization of wine, brandy, and tobacco enterprises in a political fight that brought down a government. (Eventually, despite communist opposition, the privatization took place and the IMF relationship was restored.[44]) The Indonesian government declared in January of 2003 that it would break free from its commitments to the IMF; parliamentary pressure, including a decree in October of 2002 requiring the government not to extend the current IMF program, was a vital part of this decision.[45]

Some developing country parliamentarians are looking to find ways to systematically become proactive, rather than merely reacting to IMF-Executive Branch agreements post hoc. In the Brazilian parliament there have been recent calls for a parliamentary front on the IMF and World Bank to heighten their accountability to parliaments across Latin America. The measures proposed include involving parliament in the selection and accountability of Brazilian representatives on the board, enacting legislation to ensure that information on loan agreements is made public, and creating mechanisms to facilitate greater participation of officials and civil society in the design of programs.[46]

The involvement of Southern country parliaments in considering, implementing, and overseeing IMF programs is circumscribed by a number of factors. Most important is the weak capacity of many of these bodies. Many Southern country parliamentarians lack the office space and paid staff needed to conduct the research required to arrive at informed assessments of these programs, let alone an independent research agency along the lines of the US Congress's General Accounting Office. Another important barrier is the reluctance of governments to involve their parliaments in these matters. By keeping parliament in the dark on the IMF program and the economic facts surrounding it, a

---

[42] Marcela Valente, 'Argentina: Economy Minister Abandons a Sinking Ship', *Inter Press Service*, 23 April 2002.

[43] 'Politics Cloud the Economic Horizon', *Middle East Economic Digest*, 7 August 1998, p. 7.

[44] 'Moldovan Government Resigns', *Deutsche Presse-Agentur*, 9 November 1999. 'Moldova 'May Face Default' After Parliament Rejects Privatization', *BBC Worldwide Monitoring*, 18 April 2000.

[45] Smitha Francis, 'Indonesia's Battle of Will with the IMF', *Network Ideas*, 25 February 2003, www.networkideas.org/themes/trade/feb2003/tp25_Indonesia.htm.

[46] www.rbrasil.org.br/frenteparlamentar.

government may hope to deflect criticism of its own failings onto the IMF and prevent parliamentarians from winning easy political victories. Finally, until recently the IMF tended to treat recalcitrant parliaments as a part of the problem or an obstacle to reform rather than as a vital source of ownership – and even authorship – of a country's economic policies.

IMF Responses

In two ways, the IMF has taken steps to enable parliamentarians to play a more constructive role. First is the broad progress over the past decade on IMF transparency. An impressive variety of important documents is now routinely released, ranging from staff reports to Letters of Intent, unless the relevant member country objects to publication.[47] Those releases go a long way toward enabling parliamentarians to understand and assess the work of the IMF. But because they rarely include documents related to issues still under negotiation, the releases do not allow for effective input into that work.

The IMF is also making quite specific efforts to inform and engage parliamentarians as part of its broader efforts encouraging governments and IMF staff (where the government allows) to reach out to a broad range of stakeholders (including parliamentarians) to build support for economic reforms. IMF missions, including those conducting Article IV surveillance, often meet with a wide range of stakeholders, not just the finance and central bank officials who have long been the Fund's interlocutors.

The IMF's resident representatives in many countries have also begun to make contact with members of parliaments. Their ability to do so depends both on their personal proclivities and on the receptivity of their host country to the idea. When it works well, such outreach can be highly productive for all concerned. In Hungary and the Czech Republic in the 1990s, for example, the resident representative met with parliamentarians as he or they saw fit. IMF missions also had regular exchanges with relevant parliamentary committees, organized by the central government authorities. Such contacts could help to give the IMF a sense of

---

47 See Publication Policies of the Fund, 12 February 2004, at www.imf.org/external/np/pdr/trans/2004/021204.pdf. IMF staff seem willing to go farther than the Executive Board will allow: see The Fund's Transparency Policy: Issues and Next Steps, at www.imf.org/external/np/pdr/trans/2003/092903.htm. See also The Fund's Transparency Policy: Review of the Experience and Next Steps, at www.imf.org/external/np/pdr/trans/2003/092903.htm. For an assessment of the Fund's disclosure policy, see the regular columns by journalist Toby McIntosh at www.freedominfo.org/ifti/imf.htm. In some cases, the IMF forbids its member governments to share certain documents even with legislators, a policy that would seem to be at odds with broader Fund interests in legitimizing decision making. See: William E. Holder, 'Publication Policies of the Fund' (Preliminary Version), IMF Legal Department and IMF Institute Seminar on Current Developments in Monetary and Financial Law, 7 May 2002. It was formerly available at www.imf.org/external/np/leg/sem/2002/cdmfl/eng/holder.pdf, but that link now goes directly to the main IMF website.

the political implications of the issues countries are facing, to identify what economically advisable steps would be politically feasible and to determine country priorities. That said, for the IMF to benefit from these contacts, the institution must find ways to incorporate the information into their operations and to feed it back to the management and staff in Washington DC.

In addition to such outreach, the Fund has begun holding seminars for parliamentarians. From 1993 to 1996, the IMF held several seminars and briefings in national capitals for policy makers from formerly communist countries of Europe and Central Asia, but these drew few legislators. In the mid-1990s, the Fund held a special seminar for Russian parliamentarians for three days at the IMF's regular training ground in Vienna. Thereafter, the Fund held several week-long sessions for parliamentarians from the region, aimed at both educating parliamentarians about the IMF's role (globally and in particular countries) and at providing an opportunity for legislators to express their views to the IMF. More recently, other seminars have been held in Africa, in Kenya in 2002, and in Ghana and Cameroon in 2003.

The Fund has also piggy-backed on the efforts of its sister institution, the World Bank, in outreach to parliamentarians. In May 2000, the European Vice-Presidency of the World Bank organized a conference in The Hague to provide a forum for information sharing and open discussion between the Bank and legislators. Out of that meeting grew what has now become the Parliamentary Network on the World Bank (PNoWB), an independent non-profit association registered under French law that brings together some 140 members of parliaments from some 60 countries. Its purpose, according to its website, is 'to increase parliamentary involvement and effectiveness in the field of international development and to encourage dialogue between MPs [members of parliament] and the World Bank'.[48] At the group's fourth annual conference, held in Athens in March 2003, IMF Managing Director Horst Kohler met with the group for a 90-minute session that involved some fairly pointed questioning about the IMF, its role, and its openness to parliamentary oversight and participation. That discussion led to an exchange of letters between the PNoWB's Africa group and Kohler, all of which are publicly available on the PNoWB website (www.pnowb.org) and the IMF website (www.imf.org). The Fund is also participating in PNoWB-sponsored visits by parliamentarians to PRSP countries.[49]

Most Executive Directors talk at least occasionally with legislators from the countries that appoint or elect them. The number and nature of such contacts vary widely, depending on the countries concerned, although most EDs report growing interest from parliamentarians in initiating such contacts. In an effort to systematize this somewhat haphazard set of interactions, in 2003 the Executive Board set up a Working Group of IMF Executive Directors on Enhancing Communication with National Legislators. Their report describes and encourages

---

48 www.pnowb.org/html/index.php?module=htmlpages&func=display&pid=1.

49 International Monetary Fund, 'A Review of the Fund's External Communications Strategy', 13 February 2003, p. 22.

more of the kinds of IMF outreach outlined above.[50] But it is very tentative on the question of just what greater parliamentary involvement should accomplish. The report argues that more dialogue would be helpful both as a way to inform parliamentarians and to enable the IMF to understand better the concerns of those legislators. But it stresses repeatedly the importance of making clear that any dialogue is *not* an opportunity for legislators to engage in program negotiations.

Parliaments as Stakeholders

As Fund staff and executive directors are quick to stress, the main role for parliamentarians is at home, overseeing their central governments, including their finance ministries, representing the interests of various constituencies, and setting their country's policies in law. Domestic politics and lack of capacity often combine to make such oversight and involvement a challenge.

One area in which the World Bank and the IMF have tried to encourage broad political support for good economic policy is in the Poverty Reduction Strategy Papers (PRSP) process that now accompanies debt relief. PRSPs describe the macroeconomic, structural, and social policies that a country intends to pursue in order to fight poverty and encourage growth. The documents are supposed to be prepared by low-income member countries by means of a participatory process that involves a wide range of interested parties within the country as well as funders, including the Bank and the Fund.[51]

Clearly, parliamentarians ought to be among the key stakeholders included in the PRSP process. But in practice, they are not. The official Bank/Fund review of the early PRSP process noted that the 'role of parliaments ... has generally been limited, although individual parliamentarians have been involved in some countries'.[52] The report notes that in just a few cases (Burkina Faso and Mauritania) have parliaments approved PRSPs, while in others (Nicaragua and Honduras) individual legislators were involved in PRSP consultations. The problem has been widely noted and funders are working to help parliaments understand the PRSP process better and participate in it more effectively. But it is clear that the PRSP process is very far from providing an answer to the problem of adequate legislative oversight of and involvement in the development process generally, much less specific oversight of Fund programs.

More generally, efforts to involve national parliaments in the oversight and monitoring of government budgets and expenditures have been very slow to

---

[50] Report of the Working Group of IMF Executive Directors on Enhancing Communication with National Legislators, 15 January 2004, www.imf.org/external/np/ed/2004/ecnl/index.htm.

[51] International Monetary Fund, 'Poverty Reduction Strategy Papers: A Factsheet', April 2003, www.imf.org/external/np/esr/facts/prsp.htm.

[52] International Development Association and International Monetary Fund, 'Review of the Poverty Reduction Strategy Paper (PRSP) Approach: Early Experience with Interim PRSPs and Full PRSPs', 26 March 2002, www.worldbank.org/poverty/strategies/review/earlyexp.pdf, p. 22.

show results and this bears directly on the role of parliaments in holding the IMF to account. Even in countries such as Uganda, Bolivia and Ghana where efforts have been made to strengthen the transparency and monitoring of public expenditure, the role of parliaments in the process has remained fairly weak.[53] This poses several challenges for the IMF.

Challenges for the Fund

Parliaments and civil society groups have for a long time eschewed or been denied a strong role in monitoring, let alone formulating, the core elements of an IMF agreement – government budgets and expenditures. If parliaments are to play a greater role, both the IMF and national governments will need at least to permit, if not to facilitate or require, parliaments to get involved. In turn, other actors will have to monitor what parliaments do in this regard.

For the IMF there is no quick or easy solution. In program countries (i.e. those that are currently receiving IMF loans) the IMF now makes substantial efforts to talk to a wider range of domestic actors, but it is still the case that the loan terms are negotiated primarily with the finance ministry. On this point, the IMF staff has no discretion – the Articles of Agreement that created the Fund specify that finance ministries and central banks are to be its interlocutors in national governments. In most cases parliaments do not get to vote on, and sometimes do not even see, the loan terms before the deal is struck. However, in most cases parliamentary approval is required to pass legislation implementing reforms and it is at least here that parliaments can and should play a constructive role. Other government institutions can help in this. For example, in many Commonwealth countries an auditor-general is required to report to parliament on government expenditures and financial and administrative actions. In Uganda, for example, the Public Accounts Committee scrutinises and comments on the auditor-general's report with some alacrity. In Ghana MPs are taking a deeper interest in monitoring the governments' expenditure and poverty-reduction policies, and in Burkina Faso the National Assembly's committees have a history of conducting enquiries on specific issues.[54] Parliaments could more actively use this kind of report, extended to cover all IMF activities in a country, as a means to hold their government to account in relations with the IMF.

A further role the IMF can play relates to the problems of 'capacity' and 'interest' often invoked to explain the lack of parliamentary input and accountability. In the Vienna seminars described above, Fund staff relate that some of the early sessions had to be devoted to explaining such basic economic facts as the tendency for large increases in the money supply (i.e. running the government printing press) to lead to inflation. There is an obvious role for the IMF to play in informing, explaining, and communicating information about economic policy. Indeed the IMF has taken to this with some enthusiasm. That said, there is a high

[53] John Roberts, *Managing Public Expenditure for Development Results and Poverty Reduction*, Overseas Development Institute Working Paper 203 (London, 2003).

[54] Ibid, p. 59.

degree of scepticism among parliamentarians, in both North and South, about the impartiality of the Fund's efforts in this regard. On the ground the Fund is often perceived as presenting just one view of economic policy or 'explaining Fund policy' rather than opening up debates about economic policy which educate and stimulate parliamentary debates and scrutiny.

Conclusions and Recommendations

The experience of creditor country parliamentary oversight of the IMF highlights several advantages and disadvantages of democratizing the Fund in this way. On the positive side, a greater engagement by parliaments could be reassuring to citizens concerned that global institutions like the IMF are out of control, providing them with a mechanism for being heard. On the global stage, as parliaments from a larger number of countries become involved, they will counterbalance the otherwise disproportionate influence of the US. Finally, as the example of the military audits indicates, parliaments can expand the IMF (board and staff) understanding of what constitutes relevant and important issues.

All that said, expanding the role of parliaments will not be a painless process. It increases the risk (although, we argue, not by much) of burdening Executive Board meetings with legislatively mandated pro forma statements and voting restrictions and eroding the deliberative, consensus-building quality of the institution. More generally, increasing the role of parliaments highlights inequalities among legislatures of different countries. Some have weak constitutional powers, few resources, or little power within domestic government. These parliaments are unlikely to be able to exert any real influence in the Fund and this could exacerbate the problem of disproportionate creditor influence in the IMF, at least in the short term. Greater participation by parliaments will bring with it all the glories of democracy, including the fact that democratic processes are invariably messy, inefficient, and time-consuming – in short, the worst form of government except for any other.

The approach we propose towards democratizing the IMF builds upon the IMF's own revolution in transparency and disclosure. Where ten years ago almost all Fund documents were difficult to obtain, today many are posted on the institution's website. Furthermore, the institution has worked proactively with all of its member governments to encourage them to be more transparent and to permit the Fund to publish details of their agreement with the Fund and IMF reports about the country. This is a vital step towards democratic accountability. That said, it permits only a retrospective kind of accountability. By contrast, this chapter has focused on an ongoing role for parliaments in overseeing the formulation and implementation of the work of the IMF – not just in post-facto reviews.

The question then arises as to whom precisely parliaments should hold to account in the IMF and how might this be better done. Is it the Fund staff or management, or is it their country's individual Executive Director or the Executive Board as a whole? Clearly all these levels of accountability are important. We would argue that progress could be made in respect of each.

The Fund staff and management should be held to account during and after negotiations with a country, for their inputs, technical work, and impact on domestic policy. This requires an increase in transparency and access to information for appropriate parliamentary representatives throughout negotiations. On this issue, IMF staff has rightly outlined problems resulting from opening up delicate negotiation processes. Too easily, openness can become the prey of vested interests or oppositional politics.[55] That said, we are arguing for a more specific kind of opening-up where a parliamentary body or committee delegated to apprise itself of negotiations with the IMF would have access to documents (including those the Fund currently classifies as 'confidential' and not for sharing even with parliaments) throughout the process. There is ample precedent of parliamentary or Congressional committees staying apprised and informed of highly sensitive information in the areas of security and intelligence, as well as on economic issues. To push forward in this way would require parliaments within Southern countries to think carefully about how they might best structure and delegate their interaction with the Fund to a particular committee or body.

This chapter has also highlighted the need for parliaments to play more of a role in holding the Executive Board of the IMF to account. The board is the political arm of the IMF, making political judgements and decisions on the basis of technical and other advice offered by the management and staff. In theory it represents all members of the institution. In practice there are serious flaws in the chain of representation and accountability.[56] But at core, if parliaments are effectively to hold the Fund to account, it is vital that they know what decisions are being made and with whose approval or abstention. They need at the very least to know how their own government (or the Executive Director representing the group of countries that includes their own) is representing their country's interests on the board. This chapter has described the ways legislatures can demand and collect information from their own governments. Progress on this would be greatly enhanced if minutes of board meetings were published in a timely way (at best they can be viewed several years later under the IMF's archives policy).[57] More ambitiously, several commentators have proposed that voting should take place on all issues and a voting record should be kept and published.[58] Indeed, this could be taken as a natural extension of the IMF's current practice of publishing on their website a summary of board discussions.

There are several arguments made against subjecting the board to this kind of scrutiny. A first is that it would diminish rather than enhance Southern power by eliminating the need to bring small countries within a consensus. The presumption here is that small countries have an informal veto power through the

---

[55] James M. Boughton and Alex Mourmouras, *Is Policy Ownership an Operational Concept*, IMF Working Paper 02/72, 2002.

[56] These are analyzed in full by Ngaire Woods (2001) 'Making the IMF and the World Bank More Accountable', *International Affairs*, **77**(1), January.

[57] 'Archives of the IMF', May 2003 Factsheet, IMF, Washington DC.

[58] Jose De Gregorio, Barry Eichengreen, Takashito Ito and Charles Wyplocz, *An Independent and Accountable IMF* (CEPR, Geneva 1999).

operation of consensus. But this is not how decision making operates in the IMF board. Typically on any issue the 'sense of the meeting' is gauged implicitly taking into account the voting power of those around the table, and when a majority is reached that is taken as the consensus of the board. Hence, small countries have no veto power to lose through published voting records.

A second argument against published voting records is that it would erode the collegiality and professionalism of the board. Board members might be overly influenced by the need to account afterwards to those they represent outside the walls of the board. This would lead them to vote for measures that did not embody good technical judgements. This argument is easy to overstate because only eight members have their own representatives on the board who could be mandated to vote in this way. All other board members must aggregate and represent the collective interests of all their constituency countries. But more deeply, the argument takes us to the heart of why the Fund should be held to account, especially by parliaments, rather than, for example, made more independent as some have argued.[59]

The argument for an independent IMF relies on a conception of the IMF as a technical organization like a central bank. An independent central bank is collegial and insulated from political pressures and broad accountability in order to make good decisions. Its legitimacy is said to derive from the quality of its decisions or outputs, rather than the nature of its process or democratic inputs. However, the IMF today is a much broader, more political organization than a central bank, and this will still be the case even if it were to enforce the philosophy underpinning its new conditionality guidelines. The IMF engages in activities and conditionalities far beyond narrow technically measurable outputs. For this reason it needs more input legitimacy than an independent central bank, a fact already recognised in the Fund's rudimentary structure of representation. In contrast to preserving secretive collegiality, the Fund's legitimacy should be further enhanced through greater transparency and accountability of board decision making.

These are not revolutionary goals. Our proposed enhancements to parliamentary oversight of the IMF could foster broader public confidence in the institution, and could better provide the institution with the kinds of information, contacts and oversight to allow it to make good policy decisions in difficult situations. That said, ensuring accountability always requires a political struggle. The governments (or particular ministries) that currently enjoy preferential influence at the Fund are unlikely to applaud proposals which dilute that influence. Indeed, this has been amply displayed in the unwillingness of European and North American members properly to debate and concede their special privileges in respect of appointing the senior management jobs in the Fund. However, the Fund is now facing increasing demands from parliamentarians as well as non-governmental groups to be more accountable. These demands are difficult to resist not least because the board, management and staff of the IMF have for a decade been exhorting all other institutions and governments to demonstrate higher and more rigorous standards of accountability and good governance.

---

[59] Ibid.

Note 1

Experiences with the Parliamentary Network on the World Bank: A View from the Inside

Norbert Mao[60]

In 2000 a group of about 50 parliamentarians from about 30 countries gathered in The Hague for the first ever meeting between the World Bank and parliamentarians. It was a bold move. The Bretton Woods twins (World Bank and IMF) usually prefer to deal with the executive branch of the government. This was therefore a groundbreaking meeting to create a direct channel of dialogue between parliamentarians and the World Bank.

But a one-off meeting would not be able to build the trust necessary for a meaningful dialogue. An institutional framework would be required to do this. That is how the idea of forming the Parliamentary Network on the World Bank (PNoWB) came to be mooted and accepted.

The level of attendance from the World Bank showed that they took the meeting very seriously. The World Bank President, James D. Wolfensohn and the Vice President for Europe both addressed the Hague meeting giving it a very high profile. The then Dutch Minister for International Development, Ms Evaline Herfkens, herself someone who has been at the forefront of calling for reforms of the international financial institutions, gave the initiative her full blessing and authorised the first grant to fund the activities. Current Norwegian Minister for International Development, Hilde Johnson also attended and addressed the meeting.

From around the world, parliamentarians prominent in the field of international development and combating corruption were the majority in the meeting. Anyone who sees the strides that the PNoWB has made now should trace it back to that first ambitious cast.

In The Hague, we acknowledged that the World Bank was not only a bank in the strict financial sense but also a knowledge bank. This knowledge is a cumulative total of the intellectual talent that the Bank has under its beck and call and also a sum of experiences, some of it disastrous, which the Bank has accumulated over the decades. This knowledge is, however, complex and needs to

[60] Norbert Mao is a parliamentarian from Uganda and a member of the Board of the Parliamentary Network on the World Bank (PNoWB).

be interpreted in order for it to be palatable to the grassroots who need it badly. We agreed that parliamentarians could act as step-down transformers for this high voltage knowledge.

The PNoWB is also a salad bowl that brings together parliamentarians from underdeveloped countries and developed countries. The interests of parliamentarians from borrower countries and donor countries cannot be identical. This diversity of worldviews and interests had to be reflected in the organisation. But even within this diversity, there is an intersection of common interests. One of these is to ensure that the International Financial Institutions (IFIs) do a good job by addressing the real needs of the people that the parliamentarians represent. These common interests can only be identified and pursued if there is a forum where the contentious issues are thrashed out. The PNoWB therefore provides a forum for open information exchange and dialogue between parliamentarians from the North and the South. In an increasingly globalised world, the founding of the PNoWB was therefore very timely.

Most donor assistance from the developed countries is approved by their parliaments. The International Development Committees of these countries rely a great deal on information from the parliamentarians from the underdeveloped countries in order to do a better job. The PNoWB provides a formal forum for this type of exchange.

I recall that when the UK Parliamentary Committee on International Development was visiting Washington DC for meetings with the World Bank and the IMF, I gave them some information concerning the Global Fund for HIV/AIDS, Malaria and Tuberculosis, and a standoff that the local IMF office was having with the Ugandan Ministry of Health about the use of the funds. In this way people I met through PNoWB became part of an advocacy campaign for us. Later we got a clarification from the IMF Managing Director Horst Kohler that helped sort out the problem.

Since that first meeting in The Hague, the PNoWB has grown into an organisation with a membership of about 160 parliamentarians from about 60 countries. The flagship event of the organisation is the Annual Conference, which gives participants an opportunity to discuss and share experiences with World Bank officials, government officials, academics and the civil society. Highly placed government officials from Africa have addressed these meetings to voice the concerns of the most underdeveloped continent. In 2001 in London, South African Finance Minister Trevor Manuel addressed the meeting. In 2002 in Berne, Senegalese President Abdoulaye Wade addressed the meeting, making an appeal for parliamentary support for the New Partnership for Africa (NEPAD).

The PNoWB seized on the wind of change in the World Bank presided over by James Wolfensohn under the Comprehensive Development Framework (CDF) and its emphasis on a participatory approach and accountability, to develop new tools to facilitate wider consultation and accountability. The first tool is the Question and Answer (Q&A) which allows parliamentarians to forward questions directly to the World Bank and get answers (or at least replies). The terminal for the Q&A is the Pan European Dialogue office at the European Vice Presidency in Paris. The other tool is the Project Implementation Watch (PIW) through which parliamentarians can do a value-for-money audit of certain projects. During the fourth PNoWB Annual Conference in Athens the organisation agreed that through the PIW we can play a more active role in monitoring the implementation of the Millennium Development Goals (MDGs).

The PNoWB has organised field visits to Uganda, India, Burundi and Albania to assess World Bank projects there. In these visits, the delegations met with officials from the World Bank country offices and the national governments. The delegations also visited project sites to see whether indeed we are moving closer to 'a world free of poverty'.

Through the PNoWB, a core team is emerging in many parliaments around the world with people committed to the issue of fighting poverty. These parliamentarians have the most up-to-date information, which is absolutely necessary for them to be good watchdogs. But the needs of parliamentarians vary from place to place. There are parliaments that are not even connected to the internet. The PNoWB therefore has to help build the capacity of parliamentarians to participate in the great debates that shape the lives of millions.

Parliamentarians have the duty to make laws, to represent their constituents and to oversee the executive branch of the government. In their engagement with the World Bank, the parliamentarians will also continue to interact with a view to better carrying out their legislative, representative and oversight roles.

In the last two years the PNoWB has stepped up its engagement with other flagships of globalisation like the IMF and the World Trade Organization (WTO). That is why the WTO Director General came to address the Berne meeting. That is why in Athens 2003 we had an exciting Question and Answer session with both James Wolfensohn and Horst Kohler.

At its founding, there were some concerns that the PNoWB could end up being a mere fan club of the World Bank – a lap dog instead of a watchdog! But given its structure and diverse membership, the PNoWB now enjoys a credibility and visibility which puts it in a unique position to monitor the policies and actions of global development actors and to hold them accountable to a wider constituency.

Note 2

Bringing More Voices into the Policy Debate

Goh Chien Yen

Despite the limiting political backdrop and resistance to proposals for fundamental changes, there are still politically feasible and effective ways of bringing greater plurality and accountability – alternative voices – to the IMF's policy formulation process:

1. Deepen the principle of national ownership by involving the national parliaments in the key economic decisions undertaken by the executive arm of the government with the IMF. Parliament should be the focal point of national debate and discussion, and where genuine country ownership can take root. The IMF should encourage the national parliaments to adopt economic policies, and not work exclusively with the executive.

2. All loan programs of the IMF should adopt the current principles of PRSPs:

- Explicit commitment to genuine national ownership of the policies, reduced Fund usage of conditions, and greater country control;
- Greater emphasis on the social and poverty impacts of economic policies;
- Emphasis on a broad-based national participation in the formulation of policies; and
- Emphasis on result-oriented approaches in assessing effectiveness of policies, in terms of poverty reduction and engendering economic growth.

3. The independent and transparent role of the IEO of the IMF should be enhanced, covering a wide range of issues. Its work program is determined through consultations. The IEO (currently it has 13 staff members) can only focus on a few topics at a time – many of the issues are ongoing and require regular if not constant monitoring. To increase capacity and ensure timeliness, it could establish standing task groups including representatives from civil society, academia, and personnel from the relevant UN agencies.

4. Diversify expertise and exploit local knowledge and on the ground experience by increased geographical decentralization. Regionally decentralized offices should include staff from the major functional departments that design and evaluate

programs, as well as area experts. In Latin America, ECLAC is an example of successful decentralization, contributing to locally based and innovative theorizing.

5. Increase lateral entry recruitment of staff with practical policy experience in developing countries. Then policy innovations might reflect the lived institutional experiences of the developing countries. The departure from intellectual mono-cropping would be even greater if recruitment of personnel with field experience could be extended beyond the central banks and finance ministries of the South.

6. Provide another channel through which local knowledge can be introduced into the IMF thinking by increasing support for developing country researchers and investing in the expertise of developing country-based professionals. The current practice of engaging the expertise of outside consultants and contracted research draws heavily on elite US academic institutions, reinforcing the paradigms and presumptions already in place within the organization itself.

7. Diversify the policy discourse by greater involvement of the UN system in areas of common concerns. Staff from UN agencies (FAO, UNICEF, UNIFEM, UNDP, UNCTAD, WHO, for example), could play a role as independent auditors, offering assessment and alternatives early in the policy formulation process.

Chapter 3

Power without Responsibility? Enhancing Learning and Policy Accountability at the International Monetary Fund[1]

Angela Wood

One of the important distinctions between ideology and science is that science recognises the limitations on what one knows. There is always uncertainty. By contrast, the IMF never likes to discuss the uncertainties associated with the policies that it recommends, but rather, likes to project an image of being infallible. This posture and mind-set makes it difficult for it to learn from past mistakes – how can it learn from those mistakes if it can't admit them? (Joseph Stiglitz, 2002).

[S]low absorption of lessons and broader policy guidance into actual operations on a systematic basis contributed to weaknesses in program effectiveness (IEO, 2002).

The sharing of information is essential for sustainable development. It stimulates public debate on and broadens understanding of development issues, and enhances transparency and accountability in the development process (James Wolfensohn, World Bank, 2001).

Calls for IMF accountability have amplified as its influence has extended deeper into areas of national policy. At issue is the policy conditionality attached to its lending. Many critics perceive that the IMF fails to properly consider the significant negative consequences that its policy prescriptions have on vulnerable groups. Others argue that the IMF's prescriptions are unable to achieve its new and broadening objectives, which include growth and poverty reduction, or that the IMF is usurping national processes and imposing its sovereignty against the wishes of many groups in society.

Critics' demands for accountability reflect the perception that the IMF has not properly reconsidered and reoriented its policies in the light of its new

[1] Thank you to Jenny Richmond, Rosemary McGee, Kees Biekart, Ben Pollard, Leslie Kenny and Caroline Robb for comments on earlier drafts of this chapter. Thanks also to Goh Chien Yen for additional quotes.

objectives, it does not heed the arguments and concerns of governments and civil society when formulating policy prescriptions, and that it does not learn from or even recognise past policy mistakes. Thus, despite a growing body of evidence, the IMF appears to continue to pursue a set of policies apparently inappropriate to many developing countries' needs, priorities, institutional sophistication and capacity, and outside the bounds of its expertise.

Critics hold the IMF accountable for policy choices because of its financial leverage, and because under the guise of its superior 'technical know-how' it is able to impose policies on weaker governments (maybe only temporarily but sometimes permanently) against their wishes and often those of their citizens too. The perception is that the IMF continues to impose inappropriate or politically unacceptable policies because the Executive Board and the management and staff bear none of the burden of failed policy or the political consequences of imposing policies against the electorate's will.

Governments are held to account at the ballot box, and dismissals (or resignations) of ministers and other senior staff are regularly meted out as a means of dealing with policy failings and public dissatisfaction. However, the IMF's political leaders and senior managers do not face these political checks and balances. Nor has civil society recourse to national legal systems since, being an international institution, the IMF has legal immunity.

The underlying issue appears to be a lack of (or inappropriate) mechanisms and incentives for staff to learn from the experience of policy application on the ground in order to improve their policy advice, and to engage with a broad range of stakeholders to consider policy options. Poor policy decisions are symptomatic of the lack of widespread debate about policy alternatives. There is a lack of inclusive, transparent mechanisms to systematically assess the outcomes of policy prescriptions prior to implementation and to evaluate them after implementation. To encourage better decision making and thus better outcomes, it is necessary to establish an effective learning culture (with incentive mechanisms).

This chapter demonstrates the need for an integrated learning and accountability mechanism to facilitate decision making at the national level, to provide a foundation for evidence-based policy making and to enhance transparency and accountability. It proposes a virtuous circle of inclusive ex ante analysis, monitoring and ex post evaluation.

First we reveal the difficulty of determining who should be accountable for policy decisions. It is argued that the government should make and be responsible for policy choices. This implies that the IMF's role should be one of policy advisor not negotiator. Second we argue that improving the quality of the IMF's advice is essential. As a public institution, whose principal function is to provide advice, the IMF should be able to account for the quality of its advice. We point to a lack of systematic policy analysis and evaluation at the IMF, and argue that to facilitate improvement a focus on results is necessary. Then we present a framework for systematic learning and evaluation based on ex ante analysis, monitoring, and evaluation. We propose that these processes should be participatory to facilitate learning both at the IMF and at the national level. We suggest that such a framework complements and can be built into the Poverty Reduction Strategy process. Appropriate incentives need to be put in place to encourage staff to effectively engage in such a process.

Policy Ownership: Who Is and Should Be Accountable?

Although the IMF is regarded as a lending institution, its main activity is to provide policy advice to governments through research and publications, technical assistance, surveillance of members' economies, and when negotiating programs attached to IMF loans. Its advisory role is most significant in relation to this latter function since by giving a 'seal of approval' and through the use of loan conditions, it has the power to considerably influence (many would argue impose) government policies.

However, there are numerous concerns about the suitability of the IMF's policy prescriptions, these include:

- Lack of appreciation of the political environment in which decisions are taken and/or to allow for it in policy advice;
- Lack of attention to the differences between countries when giving advice;
- Advising policies that are not institutionally feasible, and failing to assess and improve governments' implementation capacity;
- Lack of understanding of the redistributive effects of some policy measures, or the need to take these into account;
- Institutional incentives to 'over-promise' on the speed at which core reforms can be implemented and longer-term sustainability attained;
- Insufficient assessment of the real economy responses to programs and to the sources of growth;
- Failure to develop strategies to respond to inevitable uncertainties about the economic environment in developing countries leading to ad hoc policy corrections;
- Inability to step back and reconsider the overall strategy pursued by programs while learning lessons from experience; and
- Inability to reorient policy advice in the light of new objectives.

If the IMF's policy prescriptions were considered to be broadly successful and pain-free then there would be little demand for accountability and both governments and the IMF would be happy to claim responsibility for them. The demand arises because some groups in society consider themselves to be adversely affected, both in the short and long-term. The problem for these groups is that IMF programs are determined outside national processes, which means it is not clear whether the government or the IMF is setting policy and, therefore, who is accountable. Moreover, it means that society's views are often not taken into consideration in the policy setting process. This lack of transparency means that both governments and the IMF can avoid taking responsibility for decisions taken.

The IMF is able to distance itself from taking responsibility for the consequences of its policy advice by claiming government 'ownership' of policies. Ownership implies that a government accepts the need for and willingly implements necessary reforms. It also implies that a government takes the decision to implement the policies specified in IMF program documents. This implies that the government is accountable for any misjudgement of policy; the IMF is simply an advisor in the background.

However, governments often have little choice but to agree to an IMF program and the IMF is by no means a passive advisor. Indeed, the IMF regards itself as an enforcer of policy change. The 1998 External Evaluation of the Enhanced Structural Adjustment Facility (ESAF) heard from developing country officials that the IMF had an 'inflexible attitude' and that the IMF often 'came to negotiations with fixed positions so that agreement was usually only possible through compromises in which the country negotiating teams moved to the Fund's positions'.[2] This raises some tricky questions about accountability. For example, ActionAid (2002) found that IMF documents revealed that the government of Malawi had been unwilling to implement aspects of its agricultural liberalisation program, but had reluctantly done so to access balance of payments support. ActionAid concluded that the government's 'willingness to accept inappropriate policy reforms in the final instance and an inability to formulate policy alternatives makes them equally responsible [as the IMF for subsequent outcomes]'.[3]

Typically, governments with good analytical capacity are in a better position to advocate their own policies and negotiate with the IMF, and therefore may have greater ownership. Conversely, where capacity is limited, the IMF's advice is more influential (Buira 2002). This capacity is often in short supply in the poorest countries, thus even when new processes are intended to facilitate government ownership the IMF remains extremely influential. For example, the content of the programs financed through the IMF's Poverty Reduction and Growth Facility (PRGF) should be derived from a government's Poverty Reduction Strategy (PRS). Thus, implicitly the government should have ownership of the PRGF program. However, in practice, 'the latter [PRSs] often set out macroeconomic policies solely in broad terms, and quantitative frameworks are typically skeletal, perhaps reflecting capacity constraints in some countries. This leaves a substantial amount of detail to be filled in by the PRGF supported program'.[4] In these cases, 'the PRGF-supported program, while consistent with the I-PRSP/PRSP, is necessarily linked to these documents only at that general level'.[5]

Government ownership is also limited by a weak bargaining position because often they cannot borrow from other sources. Since the IMF 'owns' the resources, it sets the policy agenda. In a meeting discussing the subject of conditionality and ownership co-organised by the IMF in 2001, Chaturon Chaisang, Minister in the Prime Minister's Office of Thailand, argued that 'in

[2] IMF, 1998.
[3] ActionAid, 2002.
[4] IMF, 2002a.
[5] IMF, 2002b.

practice, adjustment programs were designed by the IMF, while the sovereign government, facing an imminent crisis, had few options other than to accept them. As such, the real "owner" of an adjustment program was the IMF, though this was seldom explicit; while the government, not the IMF, would be held accountable for a program's failure. In his view, therefore, the IMF should be prepared to share the responsibility for the consequences of the programs it supported'.[6]

The IMF's leverage is increased by the fact that a government must agree to a program with the IMF as a 'seal of approval' to release resources from other donors: 'a number of Senegalese officials who have participated in negotiations with the IMF over time thought that the level of "country ownership" of programs has generally been low. In their view, the seal of approval role of IMF arrangements in unlocking other sources of financing gave the IMF the upper hand in negotiations with the authorities, and that sometimes the authorities went along with these proposals – even though they had doubts about their ability to deliver on implementation – in order to secure urgently needed resources.'[7]

Of course governments may sometimes overstate their lack of ownership to avoid accountability for policies. In some cases governments have been able to hide behind IMF conditionality and push the blame for difficult reforms on to the Fund (Boughton, 2003). Thus governments have avoided accountability for reforms that they would probably have implemented in the absence of conditionality. In other cases some governments have been able to justify repeated reversal of reforms and the confusion and instability this causes by claiming they were imposed by the IMF, and so continue with and even garner greater support for ineffective or even harmful 'national' policies (Collier, 2000). Both cases are dysfunctional. For countries that are in a long-term borrowing relationship with the IMF, the IEO concludes that 'there is an inherent tension between quasi-permanent conditionality, implicit in prolonged use, and country "ownership", in the sense of countries taking responsibility for the conduct of their economic policy, both by being in the driver's seat and by facing the consequences of their decisions'.[8]

Usually, both governments and the IMF have a degree of ownership. However, judging who should be accountable for particular policy impacts is made problematic by the closed nature of negotiations. It is difficult to determine which policy choices are taken independently of the IMF's advice, which are influenced by it and which are imposed.

Judging who in the IMF is responsible and, therefore, accountable for policy decisions, and who should hold them to account is also problematic. While IMF staff negotiates programs directly with government staff, Executive Directors (EDs) sitting on the IMF's Executive Board can also be influential in determining a program's content. The staff impose their technical judgements and the board its political priorities, but it is not made clear in program documents to who in the IMF policy should be attributed. While the Managing Director gives initial approval to a program the board gives final approval.

---

[6] DSE, 2001.
[7] IEO, 2002.
[8] IEO, 2002, p. 81.

The IEO (2002) argues that technical judgements should be clearly distinguished from political judgements. The latter should be made in a transparent manner at the level of the Managing Director and the board who should be accountable for them. However, while the board oversees and can hold to account the management and staff, there is no effective mechanism to hold the board to account.

The Board of Governors, which appoints the Executive Board, and the International Monetary and Finance Committee, which provides some policy direction to it, meet only once and twice a year respectively. Consequently they have little effective capacity to oversee the Executive Board as a whole. At the country level, each governor only has oversight of the ED who represents his/her country – for those in multi-country constituencies this can be minimal – and no oversight of an ED appointed/elected by another constituency. Thus those countries with minimal voting power have little influence on the decision making process and minimal capacity to exercise oversight. Moreover as Eggers, Florini and Woods point out, the decisions of individual board members are not known since there is no formal vote taking and their positions are not made public, which limits the possibility for parliamentary scrutiny of board decisions and their ED's role.

There are two options for improving policy accountability. The first is to make transparent who, amongst the government and within the IMF, has taken and is responsible for a policy decision and what that decision is. In Chapter 4, Bradlow explores the case for introducing operational policies and procedures as a means of establishing accountability and an ombudsman to enforce them. Establishing clear, transparent procedures for program negotiations could be helpful to determine responsibility for decisions made.[9]

A requirement of an operational procedure for policy negotiations could be that the IMF should state its negotiating position publicly at the start of program discussions. This could be achieved by publishing the staff's mission briefs, which form the basis of negotiations with governments. At present these are not even revealed to the IMF's Executive Board. Chaturon Chaisang, Minister in the Prime Minister's Office of Thailand, has proposed that program documents should clearly indicate which policies have been adopted on the IMF's advice/insistence and which are desired by the government. However, he notes that 'such a model would no doubt raise political and diplomatic sensitivities'.[10] It could also give inappropriate or confusing signals to markets and political stakeholders. A third element could be to make program documents publicly available within the country in draft form, giving an opportunity for parliament to scrutinise them prior to the government signing. This has been proposed by the IMF staff but has not been taken forward by the Executive Board.

---

[9] The External Evaluation of ESAF (1998) noted that ministers and government staff found that the flexibility of mission leaders during negotiations depended very much on personal factors and the extent to which they felt confident of the support of various departments at the IMF's headquarters. Many ministers felt that too much depended on these factors and that the negotiation processes would be greatly facilitated if some institutional safeguards were found for reducing them.

[10] DSE, 2001.

A second option is to allow governments to choose their preferred policy routes for which they are fully accountable and to scale back the IMF's remit to an advisory function. Chautran Chaisang argues that 'In such a model [of national ownership], the IMF would provide resources without conditionality and simply monitor progress under the (government's) program. The IMF staff could give policy advice which the government would be free to ignore, but if the program failed, the government alone would have to take responsibility'.[11]

Adopting an advisory function rather than a negotiating function would not necessarily reduce the IMF's influence and may even increase it. The IMF argues that policy conditionality ensures that governments carry out necessary reforms in order to stabilise their economies. However, policy conditionality does not ensure this. It is often not implemented or is quickly reversed and, therefore, is largely ineffective at inducing long-term, sustainable reform (Collier, 2000; Burnside and Dollar, 1998; Dollar and Svensson 1998; Devarajan *et al.*, 2001; IEO, 2002; Ivanova *et al.*, 2003; Killick, 1998; World Bank, 1998).[12] In contrast, Gunning (2000) suggests that governments are receptive in the early stages of program discussion to policy advice.

Allowing governments to make their own policy choices does not mean that no conditionality could or should be applied. An alternative could be for the government, the IMF, and other stakeholders to jointly agree on a limited set of outcome targets (performance indicators) for program monitoring. Not only would outcome conditionality help to give back policy responsibility to governments, it would allow them to seek advice from other sources. Bringing some competition into the provision of macroeconomic policy advice could help to improve it by giving incentive to providers to ensure that their advice is more finely tuned to a government's priorities, political circumstances and capacities, and to evaluate its impact.[13]

---

[11] DSE, 2001.

[12] Buira (2002) argues that it is the incentive to maintain access to future lending that gives incentive to governments to repay the IMF's loans. Policy conditionality is unable to do this since it is only effective while the program is active, yet repayments must continue to be made several years later.

[13] Since the IMF faces little or no policy competition, this has allowed the IMF to focus on how to make its conditionality tool more effective at inducing reform rather than focusing on improving the policy content. The conditionality streamlining process initiated in 2001 was largely such an initiative. It did not consider why it was that its policy prescriptions have so regularly been ignored or reversed. To the extent that conditions were not implemented because there were too many and some were regarded as unnecessary, then the streamlining process may be useful. However, the fact that conditions are implemented but later reversed suggests that it is not just the quantity but also the quality of the conditions that is at issue, implying that the IMF's advice is not convincing to governments. Some competition might encourage the IMF to look more closely at this issue.

Assessing the Quality of the IMF's Advice

A second aspect of accountability is to assess on what basis decisions have been taken, and whether they have been effective in achieving their intended outcomes. It is argued that IMF staff cannot be held to account in any punitive sense for poor policy outcomes since outcomes can be affected by many factors beyond their control. Moreover, their policy advice is only as good as the data they receive from governments. However, regardless of whether or not the IMF continues to negotiate programs or scales back its influence to that of an advisor, as a public institution, the IMF has a duty to demonstrate the quality and effectiveness of its advice. Its staff should be able to account for why they have proposed particular reforms, demonstrate on what evidence their advice is based and what they expect the results to be, and their performance assessed accordingly. This implies the need for a much more transparent process of policy formulation and a more concerted focus on results.

Evaluations carried out by the IMF's Independent Evaluation Office (IEO)[14] point to several shortcomings in the IMF's policy development processes, which call into question whether the advice it gives is optimal. However, a lack of analytical detail in program documents makes it difficult to assess on what basis the IMF's policy prescriptions have been formed.

Firstly, program documents do not reveal what the staff perceives the problem to be, and therefore, what it is that their advice is intended to address. Neither is it clear on what assumptions their advice is based, nor how the policy is expected to operate through the economy to achieve its objectives. The rationale is obviously understood internally but it is not made explicit in program documents, thus it cannot be assessed (IEO 2003a).

Secondly, poor policy advice can result from over-optimistic projections of key outcomes. Reviewing IMF policy advice to Korea, Indonesia and Brazil, the IEO found that 'macroeconomic outcomes turned out to be very different from program projections. In Indonesia and Korea, the initial projections were overly optimistic, leading to a design of macroeconomic policies in the programs that turned out to be too tight'.[15] Reviewing IMF fiscal policy, the IEO found a 'reluctance to predict a downturn [in growth]' which has 'potentially significant implications for program design, since it means that the need for countercyclical fiscal policy and its appropriate role is rarely discussed explicitly'.[16]

Although it is unlikely that staff can predict outcomes exactly, it is not unreasonable to expect that they should aim to make accurate predictions with the degree of accuracy improving over-time. However, projections of key outcomes when programs are in the formulation stage tend to be persistently over-optimistic about both the speed of restoration of macroeconomic sustainability and the pace at which structural reforms can be implemented, with strong tendencies to make over-

[14] Established in 2001, the IEO provides independent evaluation of the IMF's policies and operations directly to the Executive Board.
[15] IEO, 2003b, p. 11.
[16] IEO, 2003b, p. 16.

optimistic projections for growth, export growth, investment rates, fiscal revenues and falls in inflation (IEO, 2002, 2003a; IDA and IMF, 2002).

The IEO (2002) agrees with the IMF's explanation that the staff's over-optimism is caused by 'inadequate analysis of the likely sources of growth and of the expected impact of planned policies'.[17] It is well known that the staff negotiates 'expected' outcomes with governments; however, wishful thinking is clearly not a firm foundation for realistic policy making. Institutional incentives towards optimistic outcomes lead to unrealistic policy choices. The implication is that programs are likely to go off-track, requiring policy adjustments mid-course.

Thirdly, despite the frequent need for program adjustments, over-optimism understates the threat of potential risks caused by changes in the economic environment. This results in a lack of prior consideration of how policies might need to change during the implementation phase (IEO, 2002, 2003a). The lack of attention to key risks, which are not spelled out in program documents, and the failure to conduct stress-testing exercises, means that there is rarely any consideration of a contingency strategy for dealing with uncertainties. This has 'sometimes led to ad hoc corrections that were inconsistent with long-term objectives'.[18]

Fourthly, there is a lack of attention to assessing a government's implementation capacity and the potential political impediments to implementation (IEO, 2002).[19] Governments' failure to implement reforms in full is often blamed for poorer outcomes than expected: 'growth targets/projections for low-income countries by the Fund, Bank and many development agencies have also tended to show an upward bias often based on assumptions of full implementation of key policy reforms'.[20] However, some developing country governments have pointed out that over-optimism is caused by the IMF's failure to understand their administrative capacity constraints and the political obstacles to implementing reforms. The IEO finds that the 'risks to the programs of weak political commitments were often understated' and that 'only limited attention was often paid to assessing and developing implementation capacity'.[21] It concludes that 'repeated underestimation of the obstacles to policy implementation is, in itself, a program design problem', and recommends 'strengthening the ability of IMF staff to analyse political economy issues so that a better understanding of the forces that are likely to block or enhance reforms can be taken into account in program design'.[22]

---

[17] IMF and IDA, 2002.

[18] IEO, 2002, p. 80.

[19] The OED (2001) finds a similar problem for the World Bank: 'CAEs [Country Assistance Evaluations] find a pattern of over-optimism about borrower government's receptivity to Bank advice, willingness to undertake difficult reforms, and capacity to implement recommended measures', p. xv.

[20] IDA and IMF, 2002.

[21] IEO, 2002, p. 58.

[22] IEO, 2002, p. 53.

The IEO has also identified shortcomings in the IMF's procedures for monitoring and evaluating programs, which casts doubt on the IMF's ability to assess the outcomes of its policy advice and thus to learn from its successes and failures in order to improve its advice.

The staff review is the vehicle through which the staff monitors implementation of policy conditionality. This includes monitoring structural benchmarks and indicative targets which are concerned with the implementation of structural reforms, and monitoring short-term quantitative performance criteria related to macroeconomic reforms. Often structural reforms are delayed and performance criteria are not achieved and it is typical that these targets are revised downwards. However, there is little substantive analysis in review documents as to why certain reforms are only partially implemented or some not at all, or why performance criteria need to be revised, even though understanding this is key to improving advice or informing lending decisions (IEO, 2003a).

During program reviews staff often provides useful suggestions for how programs might be better formulated. While such suggestions are often insightful, they come once the program is underway when it is unlikely that a program will be significantly revised. It is not clear why these suggestions are not being made at the program formulation stage when they could have some impact on program design (IEO, 2003a). At present there appears to be relatively little discussion of alternatives at this stage, at least not beyond the staff. No detail is provided in program documents as to which options were considered, or explanation provided as to why a particular choice was made.

Sixthly, there is no formal evaluation at the end of a program and little evidence of efforts to evaluate the previous program when preparing a new one. Although the staff argues that evaluation of outcomes is implicit in the process of negotiating a new program, this appears to amount to little more than reviewing which conditions were implemented and which were not. With respect to fiscal policy, the IEO (2003) finds that 'many program-request documents are insufficiently linked to past outcomes and past reform attempts', and that '[f]ew efforts are made to analyse the factors behind past policy failures'.[23] In particular there is little analysis of why programs go off-track or why reforms are subsequently reversed. The IEO (2002) found substantial errors and gaps in the MONA database for tracking performance under programs, especially with regard to data on outcomes. It concludes that 'existing weaknesses in data on how programs have performed are an impediment to efforts to enhance the IMF's ability to learn from experience and to monitor the implementation and impact of its own policies'.[24]

---

[23] IEO, 2003a, pp. 73, 69.

[24] The Office of Internal Audit and Inspection examines IMF operational procedures and financial reporting and reports its findings to the board; these are not made public. The Independent Evaluation Office undertakes ad hoc reports on IMF policies, program impacts and operations. The IMF's staff also undertakes ad hoc internal audits on issues to do with operational procedures and policies, which may or may not be published.

This lack of attention to monitoring outcomes can partly be explained as a hangover to earlier days when monitoring inputs was considered to be sufficient since IMF policy was related to a small number of technical actions to maintain exchange rate alignment, which was relatively easy to observe. However, today the IMF's objectives have become increasingly complex, moving beyond balance of payments stabilisation to include growth and recently poverty reduction and the Millennium Development Goals (in the poorest countries). These broader objectives are not so readily observed and require much deeper understanding of how macroeconomic and structural policies impact on wider aspects of the economy and society such as income distribution, vulnerability to price changes, and access to services. This suggests the need to reorient and improve internal monitoring and evaluation systems to focus on results in order to equip staff with the means to assess policy impacts to improve their technical advice.

Ironically, the IMF has typically shied away from evaluating the outcomes of its policy advice on the basis that outcomes are hard to determine: '[t]he problem is that it is very difficult to evaluate the effects of programs on macroeconomic variables for several reasons. First, the links between policies and outcomes is uncertain. Second, it is necessary to filter out the effects of unanticipated exogenous influences. Third, one has to define the relevant "counter-factual".'[25]

The first argument, that the links between policy inputs and outcomes is uncertain, is precisely why attention needs to be paid to evaluating outcomes. A pilot project between the government of Burkina Faso and a group of multilateral and bilateral donors in the Special Partnership with Africa (SPA), using outcome indicators (rather than input conditionality) for loan disbursement, revealed that the expected results had not materialised despite the government's good track record of policy implementation. This brought into question the donors' responsibility for their policy advice. Focusing on results enhances government ownership and changes the nature of the government-donor dialogue, making for more realistic and objective interventions (World Bank, 2000). Likewise, the World Bank's Operations Evaluation Department (OED) concludes that 'findings from project audits and country evaluations suggest that the achievement of immediate policy objectives does not necessarily translate into long-term impact on incomes and poverty'.[26]

Secondly, although unanticipated exogenous shocks are likely to send programs off-course, the IMF staff should be able to identify what the likely uncertainties are and how policies might be altered to deal with these if they materialise. As the IEO reveals, the IMF does not demonstrate in its program documents that it is taking anticipatable uncertainties into account in its policy design. Evaluation should not aim to 'filter out' uncertainties; instead the aim of evaluation should be to learn why these shocks were not anticipated so that they can be better anticipated through ex ante analysis and factored into future policy design.

Thirdly, policy outcomes do not need to be assessed against the counter factual of how an alternative policy scenario might have performed. The necessary counterfactual is the staff's assessment of the problem, their justification for the

[25] Khan, 2001.

[26] OED, 2001, p. xiv.

policy scenario they propose, their prediction of what should happen under the policy scenario in relation to key objectives and how well they assessed risks to the outcomes being achieved.

The lack of attention to results at the highest levels is the crux of the accountability issue, and feeds through into a work culture that provides poor incentives to staff to improve their policy advice. The IEO finds that 'most mission chiefs do not feel that their career progression depends significantly on whether the programs they negotiate and oversee achieve their objectives'.[27] A large proportion 'believe that their performance appraisal would be better if they were "tougher" in negotiations with countries', reflecting the impression that the IMF is more concerned with getting maximum change than with maximising policy outcomes.[28]

Moreover, staff incentives implicitly discourage deepening understanding of policy application at the country level.[29] The reward structure gives higher priority to learning how the IMF works internally, discouraging staff from staying in any one department for too long. High staff turnover 'is a significant impediment to the development of an effective learning culture, not least because many of the lessons to be learned from experience are country specific'.[30] It also limits accountability, since individual staff's contributions to the outcomes of a program become harder to assess, and staff have often moved to other departments before a program can be completed and evaluated. The IEO concludes that 'a revamping of internal personnel incentives to encourage greater stability is needed. The focus of these incentives should be tilted toward encouraging the development of a deeper familiarity with the problems of individual countries, and correspondingly increasing responsibility, through longer country assignments'.[31]

Transparent Decision Making, Accountability and Learning

The absence of an integrated, transparent system of prior analysis, performance monitoring and evaluation of outcomes at the IMF is cause for concern. It casts doubt on the IMF's ability to manage programs, learn from and improve its policy advice, and to demonstrate its effectiveness. There is an opportunity to put in place a results-based system, which not only facilitates learning at the IMF, but also helps to build on knowledge and policy making capacity at the national level. Whilst IMF learning about policy impacts is important, it is equally important that this knowledge is rooted within countries where day-to-day policy decisions are being taken, where it matters most. To maximise learning by all stakeholders, processes for policy design, decision making, monitoring, and evaluation all need to be transparent and inclusive.

---

[27] IEO, 2002, p. 68.
[28] IEO, 2002, p. 65.
[29] Country-specific knowledge is an important input into good ex ante PSIA and risk analysis (Robb, 2002).
[30] IEO, 2002, p. 68.
[31] IEO, 2002, p. 89.

What follows is an outline of how a results-based system of policy advice and evaluation might be organised and how this could facilitate improved decision making and accountability.

Policy Determination

The first step is to make explicit in program documents the logic on which the IMF has formulated its policy advice. This should include identifying what the problem is, what the immediate and long-term objective of the policy reform is, the assumptions on which the advice is based, the transition mechanism through which the reform will operate, and expected outcomes.

From a policy making perspective, transparently laying out the policy logic in this way can help to focus staff attention on the real economy responses to policy change, thereby improving staff projections and policy advice, providing a more coherent framework for sensitivity analysis, and promoting greater awareness of the risks and uncertainties involved. From an accountability perspective, it 'serves as the baseline against which to monitor performance'.[32]

In terms of getting policies right, the balance of effort should be weighted towards the design stage, since it is more difficult to change direction once a program is being implemented. Thus the range of policy options needs to be fully considered and their viability tested prior to a decision being taken.

Viability includes assessing whether the government has the capacity to implement the proposed reforms and a supportive political environment. For the poorest countries, assessment of the expected poverty and social impacts should also be undertaken. This analysis should also be reported as a necessary element of the policy logic. In addition, policies should be stress-tested, with key risks to a program identified up-front to facilitate contingency planning. Contingency plans should also address what policy changes or safety nets to implement should negative social impacts prove bigger than anticipated.

There has been considerable discussion about whether the IMF should assess political economy issues. While there are concerns that the IMF would be straying too far into the domestic political arena, the IMF is unable to offer practical solutions if it is not aware of the political climate in which a government operates, and does not understand where it faces constraints and where there is room to manoeuvre. However, the IMF's ambition should not be to make its advice 'politics proof'. It is up to governments to determine which policies are most appropriate and to justify them to their societies. Instead the IMF's aim should be to focus its advice within a country's political context and in accordance with its institutional capacities.[33] In the context of the World Bank, the Operations Evaluation Department concurs that 'development effectiveness depends critically

---

[32] World Bank, 2002.

[33] Typically the IMF tries to bend a country's political context to fit its advice. However, some political situations may be so extreme that the IMF may simply judge that it is too unsettled a climate for achieving any significant policy change, in which case it may choose not to lend.

on adapting institutional priorities and programs to individual countries' constraints and opportunities. Such adaptation requires an up-to-date knowledge base about country operating contexts and the enabling environment'.[34] The IEO (2002) argues that since the staff already implicitly assesses political feasibility, this should be made explicit in staff reports.

Poverty and Social Impact Analysis (PSIA) of policies expected to have significant social impacts is a requirement for Poverty Reduction and Growth Facility (PRGF) programs.[35] The staff is required to take PSIA into consideration and report findings in PRGF program documents (IMF, 2002).[36] PSIA is not undertaken directly by the IMF; instead it is being carried out by the World Bank and bilateral donors.

Ideally, PSIA needs to be carried out at the stage of discussing policy options if it is to contribute to evidence-based policy making. Richmond and Ladd (2002) argue that PSIA should be conducted on a range of different policy options, so that the best policy for poverty reduction can be selected.[37] However, examining initial ex ante assessments, Bretton Woods Project (2002) concludes that '[t]he pilot studies being carried out by the World Bank and DFID [Department for International Development] for the most part fail to do this [look at policy alternatives]. Instead they take single pre-existing reforms, which are assumed to be going ahead, and focus on sequencing and mitigation measures. They do not question whether or not this reform is the appropriate or optimal one for poverty reduction'.

The implication is that while PSIA may be helpful for monitoring purposes by providing an initial assessment of likely outcomes, it is not being factored into the policy process early enough to facilitate decision making between policy alternatives.

The IMF has a responsibility to fully inform governments of both the social benefits and the costs of implementing its advice prior to a decision being taken. This implies that it should be developing its capacity to determine when PSIA is necessary, that PSIA should be an integral part of its policy deliberations and therefore carried out early on, and that it should collaborate with others to undertake it.[38]

---

[34] OED, 2001, p. xiii.

[35] PSIA is the analysis of intended and unintended consequences of policy prescriptions on the well-being of different social groups, particularly the poorest and most vulnerable.

[36] For an analysis of linkages between macroeconomic policies and social and poverty impacts, plus examples of PSIA carried out in relation to IMF programs, see Robb, 2002.

[37] While the IMF/Bank process runs from policy formulation to PSIA, many outside the IMF argue that to facilitate democratic decision making the reverse is needed. The question should not be 'what impact do the prescribed policies have on society or poverty reduction?' but 'which macroeconomic and structural policies achieve the best results for poverty reduction?'. Schmidt (2002) neatly reorients the process as 'Macroeconomic Policy Impact Assessment'. The implication is that PSIA or MPIA should be carried out first leading to a policy decision, thereby facilitating policy transparency and dialogue at the national level.

[38] Selvaggio and Joyner (2002) propose that teams conducting PSIAs should include World Bank or IMF staff, members of the host country governments, civil society representatives and local experts from the country.

Program Monitoring

While the IMF has traditionally focused on monitoring program implementation, a focus on results requires monitoring whether the program's immediate objectives (outputs) are being achieved, and secondly, whether it is on course to achieve its intermediate objectives (outcomes) and longer-term goals (impacts). One means to focus the IMF's attention on monitoring outputs and outcomes as opposed to policy inputs is to switch to outcome conditionality instead of policy conditionality.[39]

In the case of the poorest countries, these longer-term goals are framed by the Millennium Development Goals. Movement towards these wider objectives will typically not be observable within the timeframe of an IMF program, implying that intermediate indicators will need to be specified. However, since the IMF's involvement in the poorest countries is often expected to be long term by having a series of rolling programs, it can also factor in monitoring the contribution of its programs to these objectives over a longer timeframe.

For monitoring results, quantitative indicators need to be selected for measuring progress towards objectives and targets. Consideration will need to be given to which indicators provide useful information towards intermediate outcomes and longer-term impacts, and which provide early-warning of the need to correct programs. For example, monitoring might want to prioritise those reforms which are anticipated to have significant social impacts (these should be identified through ex ante PSIA) or reforms identified as vulnerable to risk in the contingency strategy. Performance monitoring should thus alert program staff to the possible need to implement the contingency strategy. Internal staff evaluation should be triggered if outcomes are found to be going off-course in order to understand why this is so and whether (further) corrective action is needed, and what the implications are for the coherence of the program.

It would be beneficial if a range of national stakeholders (and donors) were involved in performance monitoring, particularly if a policy reform has a potentially large social impact or high degree of uncertainty and may need to be adjusted. For an effective collaborative process, it is essential for all parties to agree, during the policy formulation stage, on outcome targets/indicators, what data needs to be collected, and how regularly it should be monitored and analysed.

Different stakeholders will interpret results differently, particularly as much data may initially be of poor quality: 'monitoring is far from being simply a technical activity; instead it is a key part of what is a highly charged political process which involves considerable vested interests, many of whom are keen that

[39] The IMF already imposes short-term quantitative targets as macroeconomic performance criteria. However, these are often not specifically monitored in relation to long-term objectives, to determine whether they contribute to these objectives. Thus domestic borrowing may be the short-term target whereas the long-term objective is greater domestic private investment; both need to be monitored.

the true nature of the situation should be concealed as much as possible'.[40] This means that the process, and who is included in it, is particularly important.

The staff should present an analysis of the performance monitoring data in relation to planned results along with the views or contradictory interpretations from other stakeholders in the process to IMF management. This should also be made publicly available. The IMF's MONA database, used for tracking performance under programs, should be made more comprehensive, accurate, and up-to-date and publicly available, as the IEO (2002) recommends.

Ex Post Evaluation and Feedback Loops

Key elements of the program should be evaluated on completion, with a view to informing the next policy/program cycle. The IEO recommends ex post assessment of all completed or permanently interrupted programs 'to ensure that the lessons for program design are absorbed more quickly'.[41]

Evaluation could:

- Examine the relationship between outputs, outcomes and whether these have contributed to longer-term goals. These should be examined in relation to expected outcomes/targets. Where there are wide discrepancies between the two, the reason for this should be assessed;
- Focus on whether anticipated transmission mechanisms were accurately specified, and if not, assess whether the assumptions made were incorrect and what the implications are for future policy;
- Examine what unanticipated factors impacted on programs and why they were not anticipated;
- Assess why certain reforms were delayed or not implemented, and the resulting effects on the program's coherence;
- Assess the effects of any adjustments to policy made during the course of the program; and
- Take a step back from the program details and examine its coherence with the government's overall reform objectives and other donor programs.[42]

This analysis should be fed back into ex ante analysis to improve projections, consideration of transition mechanisms, risk assessment, PSIA and analysis of institutional and political capacities and to inform alternative policy options. To facilitate and demonstrate the absorption of lessons learned into future programs, staff should be required to detail in PRGF documentation and requests for the use of Fund resource documents how the proposed program has been informed by the evaluation results and discussions of these at the national level. Such a procedure is

[40] Oxfam, 2002.

[41] IEO, 2002, p. 86.

[42] The IEO (2002) argues that this could be carried out through the IMF's surveillance processes.

consistent with the IEO's (2002) recommendations that 'Staff reports ... should provide more of a perspective of the history of the IMF's program involvement with a country. This should highlight what has been achieved and where previous strategies have fallen short of their objectives and why'.

As with monitoring during implementation, evaluation of outcomes should be an open process involving IMF staff, key national stakeholders, donors and evaluation specialists, and should bring together quantitative and qualitative data from a range of sources. A participatory process is likely to generate a wider range of data, and therefore a more disaggregated picture of policy impacts (Robb, 2002). There are likely to be conflicting views of successes and failures and costs and benefits. Conflicts of interest are likely to be common and consensus rare. Evaluation should be understood as a means to negotiate these different realities, providing opportunities for program stakeholders to reconcile their various perspectives or versions of reality (Earl *et al.*, 2001). Reconciling these (or not) is an invaluable opportunity for broadening understanding. The co-existence of different interpretations of outcomes requires participants in the process to become aware of different points of view and broadens the interpretation of the evidence. This can help to avoid 'paradigm traps' among policy makers that limit their views on development options (ECPDM, 2003). The participation of all key actors is important because 'it is often the learning that takes place in the course of the evaluation process which is most used, rather than the report prepared at the end'.[43]

Performance Monitoring for Learning and Accountability

There is likely to be a trade-off between performance monitoring to improve learning and performance monitoring for accountability to internal and external stakeholders. The latter is likely to encourage a greater focus on easily measurable outputs which are more easily attained and attributed to IMF activities and for which data can be regularly collected, rather than a focus on outcomes and overall goals. Since program staff cannot easily be held accountable for outcomes that can be affected by many factors, this is also likely to encourage a focus on inputs and outputs for which staff can have (potentially) great control. Whereas performance monitoring for learning is more likely to encourage a shift in attention away from inputs and outputs to outcomes and impacts on longer term goals, and to better understanding of the cause-effect linkages between them. While accountability tends to be a backward-looking, fault finding exercise, learning takes a more positive, forward-looking perspective.

Secondly, accountability reporting is likely to require much more rigorous data collection, methodology and attention to data quality and external verification. Annual reporting may also encourage standardisation of outcome performance criteria for aggregation purposes, which may not be optimal or possible. The data/results for which it is possible, such as inputs and outputs, may not be very informative whereas learning for decision making is more likely to involve more

[43] Earl *et al.*, 2001.

rapid and low cost data collection and appraisal techniques and self-assessment, and encourage more participatory methods and stakeholder involvement.

Thirdly, accountability reporting, especially if linked to rewards or penalties, is more likely to encourage risk averse behaviour and a focus on easily achievable results or what is easily measured. In contrast, a learning approach may encourage risk-taking and experimentation (OECD, 2001).

Given these trade-offs it would seem to be more beneficial to implement a results-based process to focus on learning to improve policy advice, since minimising adverse policy outcomes and maximising goals would seem to be more worthwhile to achieve than apportioning blame.

Instead, it would seem more appropriate to allow governments to take policy decisions and for them to be held accountable at the national level. In which case staff could be appraised on the basis of how well they understand transition mechanisms and can anticipate shocks and risks into their policy analysis, whether they undertake PSIA, how willing staff are to enter into discussion with national stakeholders and comprehend different view-points during performance monitoring, and to what extent they feed evaluation experience back into their ex ante analysis and policy design, and generally how well they comply with operational procedures for preparing policy advice, and monitoring and evaluation (see next chapter).

Resources

Introducing more analysis and evaluation into program design will require more staff time and resources. Previous efforts to encourage ex-post assessment of programs have been hampered by a lack of time in busy program departments, suggesting that staff numbers should be increased in these (IEO, 2002). Departmental targets for staff time allocated to analysing monitoring and evaluation findings could be introduced to help staff prioritise competing requirements. Introducing more analysis and evaluation is also likely to require a wider range of expertise than the IMF currently employs.

Financial resources could be redirected from current surveillance budgets. A significant amount of resources (both staff and financial) are spent monitoring industrialised economies with little overall benefit (Crow *et al.*, 1999). These activities could be reduced and the freed-up resources channelled into area departments engaged in lending and program activities.

Although a results-based system will cost more, it is also likely to save money in the long-run if it leads to better policy design, better program implementation and better outcomes.

Conclusion

Accountability and effective learning are two sides of the same coin. If the IMF can demonstrate that it is learning from policy mistakes, through a transparent and systematic learning process, and taking appropriate action, then it is effectively being accountable.

However, no matter how well designed IMF policy becomes, there will always be winners and losers. Therefore, designing the 'right' policy will never be a purely technical process. Inevitably, there will be a political element to the policy choice and losers will demand accountability. Democratising decision making, by opening up policy debate at the national level and enabling decisions to be taken here, effectively 're-politicises' policy making, and allows those who take decisions to be held accountable. The implication is that the IMF should satisfy itself with a purely advisory role and should resist imposing policy conditionality.

In an advisory capacity the IMF still has a responsibility to demonstrate the outcomes of its policy advice. To improve and demonstrate the quality of its advice, the IMF needs to establish clear processes by which assumptions and policy rationale are clearly articulated, ex ante analysis of impacts and risks feeds into its policy advice, intermediate monitoring feeds into program review and ex post evaluation informs new program design to facilitate evidence-based policy making. At every stage data and analysis should be made publicly available.

The IMF has an opportunity to facilitate accountability and learning at the national level as well as for itself by including national stakeholders in monitoring and evaluation processes. Inclusive and transparent monitoring and evaluation is likely to be as equally political as making policy choices. Different stakeholders will interpret results differently and debate about policy choices will almost certainly open up areas of conflict between stakeholders. However, the opportunities for all stakeholders to learn from this process are invaluable, and efforts should be made to share lessons beyond those immediately involved in the process.

Incentive structures will need to change at the IMF to encourage staff to fully engage in such monitoring and evaluation processes. The IMF should fulfil the IEO's recommendations to assess implicit and explicit staff incentives in order to reorient these to support a culture based on performance and to facilitate learning.

This discussion has barely touched upon the issue of data problems. That data problems exist is put forward as a case for not undertaking impact analysis, monitoring and evaluation. This is a short-term issue; with due incentive the necessary data will be collected. The IMF has made it a priority to push governments to collect and publish good quality data in other areas through its Special and General Data Dissemination Standards which has given due incentive to governments. It can likewise do the same for data on outcomes and key objectives. Improving the IMF's own databases and making these public should be a priority to demonstrate that it is willing to practise what it preaches.

However, in terms of both accountability and learning, no matter how good the data, policy design and evaluation will be a political process. Thus the transparency and inclusiveness of these processes is essential. As Earl *et al.* (2001) point out, the most useful lessons are often achieved during the process rather than from the actual data. Whether the IMF is prepared to learn will depend on whether it is prepared to be accountable to a wider public.

References

ActionAid US (2002) *Death by Starvation in Malawi: The Link Between Macro-economic and Structural Policies and the Agricultural Disaster in Malawi*, Policy Brief, Washington DC, www.actionaid.org/newsandmedia/actionaid_malawi_policy_brief.doc.

Botchwey, K. *et al.* (1998) *External Evaluation of ESAF*, Report by a group of independent experts, IMF, Washington DC, www.imf.org/external/pubs/ft/extev/index.htm.

Boughton, J. (2003) *Who's In Charge? Ownership and Conditionality in IMF Supported Programs*, IMF, Washington DC, www.imf.org/external/pubs/cat/longres.cfm?sk=16796.0.

Bretton Woods Project (2002) 'Real Impact of New Poverty Analysis Uncertain', www.brettonwoodsproject.org/topic/adjustment/a3101psia.html.

Buira, Ariel (2002) 'An Analysis of Fund Conditionality', http://ksghome.harvard.edu/~.drodrik.academic.ksg/g24buira.pdf.

Burnside, C. and D. Dollar (1998) *Aid, the Incentive Regime, and Poverty Reduction*, Policy Research Department, Working Paper No.1937, World Bank, Washington DC, www.worldbank.org/html/dec/Publications/Workpapers/WPS1900series/wps1937/wps1937.pdf.

Collier, P. (2000) 'Consensus Building, Knowledge and Conditionality', http://orion.forumone.com/ABCDEfiles.fcgi/139_collier.pdf.

Crow, J. et al. (1999) *External Evaluation of IMF Surveillance*, Report by a Group of Independent Experts, IMF, Washington DC, http://www.imf.org/external/pubs/ft/extev/surv/index.htm.

Devarajan, S. *et al.* (2001) *Macroeconomic Policy and Poverty Reduction*, Chapter 6 PRSP Sourcebook, Washington DC, World Bank.

Dollar, D. and W. Easterly (1998) *The Search for the Key: Aid, Investment and Policies in Africa*, World Bank, Washington DC, www.worldbank.org/html/dec/Publications/Workpapers/wps2000series/wps2070/wps2070.pdf.

Dollar, D. and J. Svensson (1998) *What Explains the Success or Failure of Structural Adjustment Programs?*, World Bank, Washington DC, www.worldbank.org/html/dec/Publications/Workpapers/WPS1900series/wps1938/wps1938.pdf.

DSE (2001) 'Ownership and Conditionality, Summary of Discussions', www.dse.de/ef/cond/rep0801e.htm.

Earl, S. *et al.* (2001) *Outcome Mapping: Building Learning and Reflection into Development Programs*, International Development and Research Centre, Ottawa.

ECDPM (European Centre for Development Policy Management) (2003), *SWAps and Decentralisation*, www.ecdpm.org.

Gunning, J.W. (2000) 'The Reform of Aid: Conditionality, Selectivity and Ownership', www.sida.se/Sida/articles/3600-3699/3676/papgun.pdf.

IDA and IMF (2002) *Poverty Reduction Strategy Papers – Progress in Implementation* (prepared by the Staffs of the World Bank and IMF), Washington DC, http://lnweb18.worldbank.org/DCS/DevCom.nsf/(documentsattachmentsweb)/September2002EnglishDC20020016/$FILE/DC2002-0016(E)-PRSP.pdf.

IEO (2002) *Evaluation of the Prolonged Use of Fund Resources*, Washington DC, www.imf.org/external/np/ieo/2002/pu/index.htm.

IEO (2003a) *Fiscal Adjustment in IMF-Supported Countries*, Evaluation Report, Washington DC, www.imf.org/External/NP/ieo/2003/fis/index.htm.

IEO (2003b) IEO Annual Report 2003, Washington DC, www.imf.org/External/NP/ieo.

IMF (2000) External Evaluation of IMF Economic Research Activities, Report by a Group of Independent Experts, Washington DC, www.imf.org/external/pubs/ft/extev/res/index.htm.

IMF (2002) Public Information Notice (PIN) No. 02/30, Washington DC, www.imf.org/external/np/sec/pn/2002/pn0230.htm.

IMF (2002a) *Review of the Poverty Reduction and Growth Facility: Issues and Options*, Report prepared by the Policy Development and Review and Fiscal Affairs Department, approved by Teresa Ter-Minassian and Masood Ahmed, Washington DC, http://www.imf.org/External/NP/prgf/2002/021402.pdf.

IMF (2002b) *Review of the Key Features of the Poverty Reduction and Growth Facility - Staff Analyses*, Report prepared by the Policy Development and Review and Fiscal Affairs Department, approved by Teresa Ter-Minassian and Masood Ahmed, Washington DC, http://www.imf.org/External/NP/prgf/2002/031502.pdf.

IMF and IDA (2002) *Heavily Indebted Poor Countries (HIPC) Initiative: Status of Implementation*, Washington DC, http://wbln0018.worldbank.org/DCS/devcom.nsf/(documentsattachmentsweb)/September2002EnglishDC20020020/$FILE/DC2002-0020 (E)-HIPC.pdf.

Ivanova, A. *et al.* (2003) *What Determines the Implementation of IMF-Supported Programs?*, IMF Working Paper WP/03/8, Washington DC, www.imf.org/external/pubs/cat/ longres.cfm?sk=16244.0.

Khan, M. (2001) *IMF Conditionality and Country Ownership of Programs*, SANEI Lecture 29 August 2001, www.icrier.res.in/pdf/mohsin.pdf.

Killick, T. (1998) *Aid and the Political Economy of Policy Change*, London, Routledge.

Operations Evaluation Department (2001) *2000 Annual Review of Development Effectiveness: From Strategy to Results*, World Bank, Washington DC, http://lnweb18.worldbank.org/oed/oeddoclib.nsf/DocUNIDViewForJavaSearch/30E7EA3D5638367A852569FB0071C7BC?opendocument.

Organisation for Economic Cooperation and Development (2001) 'Results Based Management in the Development Cooperation Agencies: A Review of Experience, Executive Summary', www.oecd.org/dataoecd/16/25/1886519.pdf.

Oxfam GB (2002) *Influencing Poverty Reduction Strategies: A Guide*, Oxfam Policy Papers, Oxford, www.oxfam.org.uk/policy/papers/prsguide/prsguide.html.

Richmond, Jenny and Paul Ladd (2002) *Proving the Impact*, Christian Aid, London, http://poverty.worldbank.org/library/view/13042/.

Robb, C. (2002) *Poverty and Social Impact Analysis – Linking Macroeconomic Policies to Poverty Outcomes: Summary of Early Experiences*, IMF Policy Discussion Paper, Washington DC, http://poverty.worldbank.org/library/view/13870/.

Schmidt, R. (2002) *Impact Assessment for Macroeconomic Poverty Policy*, Paper prepared for the UNDP Regional Program 'Macroeconomics of Poverty Reduction'.

Selvaggio, K. and K. Joyner (2002) *Comments on 'A Users Guide to Poverty and Social Impact Analysis'* (Draft Edition) and Reports of PSIA Pilot Studies, Washington DC, http://poverty.worldbank.org/library/view/13205/.

Stiglitz, J. (2002) *Globalisation and its Discontents*, W.W. Norton and Company Ltd, New York.

Van Houtven, L. (2002) *Governance of the IMF: Decision Making, Institutional Oversight, Transparency and Accountability*, IMF, Washington DC, www.imf.org/external/pubs/ft/pam/pam53/contents.htm.

World Bank (1998) *Assessing Aid: What Works, What Doesn't, and Why?*, Oxford University Press, New York, www.worldbank.org/research/aid/aidtoc.htm.

World Bank (2000) *Conditionality Revisited: A New Approach in Burkina Faso*, PREM Notes, Economic Policy, No.35, www1.worldbank.org/prem/PREMNotes/ premnote35.pdf.

World Bank (2001) 'Structural Adjustment Retrospective, Final Report', http://lnweb18.worldbank.org/ext/language.nsf/0a70c4735d4fc79e852566390063b35c/eec155910a2720a885256ae30076a40c/$FILE/alretro.pdf.

World Bank (2002) *A Users's Guide to Poverty and Social Impact Analysis* (Draft) Washington DC, www.worldbank.org/poverty/psia/draftguide.pdf.

Chapter 4

Operational Policies and Procedures and an Ombudsman

Daniel D. Bradlow

Introduction

This chapter is about the administrative practices of a public institution, the International Monetary Fund (IMF). The principles of good governance require that the IMF's administrative practices should promote both efficient and effective IMF operations and the accountability of IMF staff and management.[1] The administrative practices can only promote accountability if they satisfy two conditions. First, the institution's stakeholders and the staff and management themselves must be able to determine if the staff and management's conduct conforms to the appropriate standards for measuring their performance. These standards can be divided into two categories. The first, which can be termed operational policies, establishes the substantive requirements that the staff and management must meet in implementing the institution's policies. Examples of operational policies are the World Bank's environmental assessment requirements[2] and the International Monetary Fund's (IMF) guidelines on conditionality.[3] The second, which can be called operational procedures, explains how the staff and management of the institution should go about making decisions and conducting its operations. Examples of operational procedures are the steps that World Bank staff must take in conducting environmental assessments[4] and the IMF's guidance note

---

[1] For a general overview of IMF governance, see, L. van Houtven, *Governance of the IMF: Decision Making, Institutional Oversight, Transparency and Accountability* (IMF Pamphlet Series #53, 2002).

[2] World Bank, Operational Manual, Volume II, 'Safeguard Policies, Operational Policy' *(OP)* 4(01), *Environmental Assessment*, 1999, http://wbln0018.worldbank.org/Institutional/Manuals/OpManual.nsf/toc2/9367A2A9D9DAEED38525672C007D0972?OpenDocument.

[3] International Monetary Fund, *Guidelines on Conditionality*, 2002, www.imf.org/External/np/pdr/cond/2002/eng/guid/092302.pdf.

[4] World Bank, Operational Manual, Volume II, Safeguard Policies, *Bank Procedure (BP) 4.01*: *Environmental Assessment*, 1999, http://wbln0018.worldbank.org/Institutional/Manuals/OpManual.nsf/ea5916efc9250d10852565af0054d273/c4241d657823fd818525672c007d096e?OpenDocument.

on the guidelines on conditionality.[5] This second category is comparable to administrative procedures in national legal systems.

The second condition is that the institution must have some mechanism for dealing with cases of staff or management non-compliance with the applicable operational policies and procedures and the consequences thereof. Examples of mechanisms established for this purpose include ombudsmen, administrative tribunals and inspection mechanisms, like the World Bank Inspection Panel.

This chapter examines how well the IMF's administrative practices conform to this principle of good governance. It is divided into four sections. The first section is a review of the existing operational policies and procedures in the IMF and a comparison with the situation in the multilateral development banks (MDBs). The second section evaluates the feasibility of the IMF establishing a comprehensive set of operational procedures. The third section considers the case for establishing a mechanism for holding the IMF staff and management accountable for their compliance with a comprehensive set of operational policies and procedures. The final section contains recommendations, based on the lessons learned in the previous sections of the chapter. It recommends that the IMF develop a comprehensive set of formal operational policies and procedures and that it establish an ombudsman to deal with the problems created by staff and management non-compliance with these policies and procedures.

The Current Situation in the IMF and Comparison with the MDBs

A. Current Situation in the IMF

Operational policies and procedures are part of the 'internal law' of an international organization. For current purposes, 'internal law' refers to the combination of the constitutive documents of the organization and the rules and regulations that it develops to govern the way in which it implements its mandate.

The IMF's internal law consists of the following:

1. *Articles of Agreement*:[6] This is the international agreement, signed and ratified by all IMF member states, that establishes the powers and mandate of the IMF. The issues addressed in the Articles include the purposes of the IMF; its powers to conduct surveillance, to provide financing to its member states and to issue SDRs; its governance structure; and the rights and obligations of IMF member states.

---

[5] International Monetary Fund, *Operational Guidance on the New Conditionality Guidelines*, www.imf.org/External/np/pdr/cond/2003/eng/050803.htm.

[6] International Monetary Fund, *Articles of Agreement of the International Monetary Fund*, adopted 22 July 1944, www.imf.org/external/pubs/ft/aa/aa.pdf.

2. *By-Laws*:[7] The Board of Governors adopts these by-laws pursuant to its authority under the Articles of Agreement. They are intended to complement the Articles. They deal with such matters as the conduct of the meetings of the Executive Board and the Board of Governors, the appointment of Executive Directors, voting, the ability of members not entitled to appoint an Executive Director to be represented at meetings of the Executive Board, budgets, audits and membership issues.
3. *Rules and Regulations*:[8] These 'provide such operating rules and procedures, regulations, and interpretations as are necessary and desirable to carry out the purposes and powers contained in the Articles, as supplemented by the By-Laws'.[9] The IMF has 20 rules and regulations, each of which is identified by letter. They cover such issues as the meetings of the Executive Board, the mechanical aspects of transactions with the IMF, accounting and reporting in the IMF, relations with non-member states, staff regulations and the operation of the SDR account. The rule dealing with staff is designated Rule-N. It covers such issues as appointment of staff, the fact that staff owe their loyalty 'entirely' to the IMF, individual staff involvement in political affairs, publications by staff, the affirmation that staff make upon their appointment, staff grievances and staff travel.
4. *Decisions of the Board*:[10] These are formal decisions of the Executive Board that establish clear policies for the IMF. They deal with such issues as the content of conditionality, Article IV consultations and the role of the IMF in governance.
5. *General Administrative Orders*:[11] These are orders issued by management. They usually deal with personnel issues as opposed to operational issues.
6. *Codes of Conduct*:[12] The IMF has a code of conduct for its staff and management and a separate code for Executive Directors, Alternate Executive Directors and their advisors. Both codes deal with ethical issues related to the problem of corruption.

---

[7] International Monetary Fund, *By-Laws of the International Monetary Fund*, adopted 16 March 1946, www.imf.org/external/pubs/ft/bl/blcon.htm.

[8] International Monetary Fund, *Rules and Regulations of the International Monetary Fund*, adopted 25 September 1946, www.imf.org/external/pubs/ft/bl/blcon.htm.

[9] International Monetary Fund, *Rules and Regulations of the International Monetary Fund*, Rule A-1, Scope of Rules and Regulations, adopted 25 September 1946, amended 1 April 1978, www.imf.org/external/pubs/ft/bl/rr01.htm.

[10] International Monetary Fund, *Selected Decisions and Selected Documents of the IMF Twenty-Seventh Issue*, 31 December 2002, www.imf.org/external/pubs/ft/sd/index.asp.

[11] International Monetary Fund, Report of the External Panel, *Review of the International Monetary Fund's Dispute Resolution System*, 27 November 2001, available at www.imf.org/external/hrd/dr/112701.pdf.

[12] International Monetary Fund, *Code of Conduct for Staff*, 31 July 1998, www.imf.org/external/hrd/code.htm; International Monetary Fund, *Code of Conduct for Members of the Executive Board of the International Monetary Fund*, 14 July 2000, www.imf.org/external/hrd/edscode.htm.

7. *Guidance Documents*: These are policy papers and guidance notes that set out the IMF's policies on specific issues. Most of these documents are operational policy documents that are intended to provide guidance on the substance of IMF policy in regard to specific activities of the IMF or to specific issues relevant to IMF operations. An example of such a document is the IMF Guidelines on Conditionality.[13] Recently, the IMF issued a guidance note that provides guidance on how the staff should implement the conditionality guidelines.[14] This is a rare example of a formal and publicly available IMF operational procedure. Most IMF operational procedures are informal and not publicly available. It is important to note that it is unclear if these guidance documents establish binding standards and procedures for IMF staff or are merely precatory in intent.

The internal law addresses four administrative issues with differing degrees of detail. The most detailed relates to the personnel policies of the IMF, including the rights and responsibilities of IMF employees. One indication of the importance that the IMF attaches to this issue is the number of mechanisms that it has established to 'enforce' these personnel policies. This infrastructure, in addition to less formal grievance procedures,[15] consists of the following elements:

1. *Ombudsmen*: Ombudsmen are able to investigate and then help resolve problems that arise between staff and management.
2. *Staff Association Committee*:[16] This is a committee of the Staff Association and one of its functions is to advise staff on their rights and responsibilities and to assist in the resolution of cases of staff grievance with IMF management.
3. *Administrative Tribunal*:[17] This is an independent tribunal on which legal experts who are not employees of the IMF serve on a part-time basis. The tribunal's function is to hear formal complaints and grievances of employees of the IMF relating to their treatment by their managers and the IMF as an institution. The tribunal has the power to overrule management and to provide complainants with compensation for the harm they have suffered and to order their reinstatement.
4. *Ethics Officer*:[18] The IMF has appointed an Ethics Officer to advise all IMF officials on issues arising from the applicable code of conduct.

---

[13] *Guidelines on Conditionality, supra*, note 3.

[14] Operational Guidance on the New Conditionality Guidelines, supra note 5.

[15] *Review of the International Monetary Fund's Dispute Resolution System*, *supra* note 11.

[16] *Review of the International Monetary Fund's Dispute Resolution System*, *supra* note 11.

[17] International Monetary Fund, *Administrative Tribunal (IMFAT)*, www.imf.org/external/imfat/index.htm.

[18] International Monetary Fund, *Ethics Officer – Terms of Reference*, 28 February 2000, www.imf.org/external/hrd/eo.htm.

These mechanisms support the internal law in three ways. First, they help educate staff about what their rights are and the standards with which they can expect their managers to conform. Second, they allow employment problems to be resolved in a way which is effective, impartial and based on the merits of the case. Third, their case records help the IMF learn lessons about the nature of the employment relationship in the institution and how to improve it.

It is important to note that the IMF has established an infrastructure for implementing its personnel law that meets almost all the requirements for accountability mentioned at the beginning of this chapter. It has clear policies and procedures, with the possible exception of a rule making process, and a mechanism for monitoring and enforcing compliance with these policies and procedures. Interestingly, this is the only part of the IMF internal law for which this observation is accurate.

The second issue addressed by the internal law is the rules and practices dealing with the governance of the IMF. These rules and practices deal with such issues as the election of Executive Directors, the conduct of Board of Governors' and Executive Board meetings, and the accounting practices of the organization.

The third issue addressed by the internal law is operational policies. The content of these policies is less detailed than the content of the law in regard to personnel matters. The mechanisms for 'enforcing' this law are also less well developed. Examples of IMF operational policies are the new conditionality guidelines,[19] and the policy documents on surveillance,[20] governance[21] and poverty reduction strategy papers (PRSPs).[22] Until recently the only IMF mechanism for monitoring compliance with these operational policies was the Policy Development and Review Department (PDR) of the IMF. It is interesting to note that PDR, whose staff are regular IMF employees, is responsible for both the development and the review of IMF policies and their implementation. There is an obvious conflict of interest between the policy development and policy review aspects of PDR's work which has tended to undermine public confidence in the objectivity of PDR reviews of IMF operational policies. Recently, the IMF, in part to address this problem, established an Independent Evaluation Office,[23] which is independent of IMF management and reports directly to the Executive Board, to evaluate selected aspects of IMF operations. Consequently, to some extent it

[19] *Guidelines on Conditionality, supra* note 3.

[20] International Monetary Fund, Public Information Notice (PIN) No. 03/50, 10 April 2003, Enhancing the Effectiveness of Surveillance: Operational Responses, the Agenda Ahead, and Next Steps, www.imf.org/external/np/sec/pn/2003/pn0350.htm; International Monetary Fund, *Surveillance: A Factsheet, April 2003*, www.imf.org/external/np/exr/facts/surv.htm.

[21] International Monetary Fund, *The Role of the IMF in Governance Issues: Guidance Note*, www.imf.org/external/np/sec/nb/1997/nb9715.htm#I2, International Monetary Fund, *Good Governance: The IMF's Role*, 1997, available at www.imf.org/external/pubs/ft/exrp/govern/govern.pdf.

[22] International Monetary Fund, *Poverty Reduction Strategy Papers (PRSP)*, last updated 16 June 2003, www.imf.org/external/np/prsp/prsp.asp.

[23] International Monetary Fund, *Independent Evaluation Office (IEO) of the IMF*, www.imf.org/external/np/ieo/index.htm.

functions as a monitor of staff and management compliance with the applicable operational policies.

The fourth and least developed area of the IMF's internal law is its formal operational procedures. Two preliminary points must be made about this area of the internal law. First, IMF 'operational procedures' can be understood as referring to the way in which the staff and management execute their responsibilities in IMF surveillance, financing, analytical, and technical assistance activities. Second, the focus of this chapter is on the establishment of formal operational procedures, which means that they have entered into force after a drafting and approval process that result in a board-level decision, and that they are publicly available.

With one exception, the IMF does not have formal operational procedures. This exception is the operational guidance note that the IMF has adopted to assist staff in implementing the conditionality guidelines.[24] The IMF does have informal procedures in the form of memoranda and notes from management to the staff that provide guidance on how they should conduct IMF operations. These existing procedures are informal in the sense that they have not been presented for board approval and are not contained in a publicly available document. One example of such an informal operational procedure, identified through references in published materials, is an operational guidance note on surveillance.[25]

The lack of formal operational policies means, for example, that there are no publicly available documents that external stakeholders can consult to learn how the IMF decides with whom it should consult during surveillance operations or in designing its financing arrangements or its technical assistance programs or in its general analytical and policy work, how it organizes these consultations, or what are the factors that staff consider in making specific types of decisions. In addition, there are no mechanisms that stakeholders can use to hold the IMF accountable for the way in which it implements the existing informal operational policies or the one formal policy. Thus, the internal law in regard to operational procedures fails to conform to either of the two standards for good administrative practices identified at the beginning of this chapter.

The IMF's failure to develop comprehensive formal operational procedures can be explained. When the IMF was responsible for managing a system of relatively fixed exchange rates, it could limit its interactions in its member states to the financial and monetary authorities. This meant that there was a limited range of officials involved in these interactions. In addition, the IMF staff would be sent on mission with detailed and carefully crafted instructions and

---

[24] *Operational Guidance on the New Conditionality Guidelines*, *supra* note 5. The IMF is currently engaged in a participatory process regarding its relations with civil society and it is possible that this process will result in a second formal operational procedure.

[25] Footnote 28 in *Enhancing the Effectiveness of Surveillance: Operational Responses, the Agenda Ahead and Next Steps*, prepared by the Policy Development and Review Department in consultation with Other Departments (13 March 2003) refers to an *Operational Guidance Note for Staff Following the 2002 Biennial Surveillance Review, September 2002.* However, this note is not publicly available.

would be required to refer matters back to headquarters before agreeing to any deviations from what was proposed in these instructions.[26] The result was that both from the IMF and the member state perspective there was limited need for formal operational procedures. Everyone involved in the discussions between the IMF and the member state knew and understood the *de facto* operational procedures.

However, following the collapse of the par value system and the expansion in the scope of IMF operations that occurred in the course of the 1980s and 1990s, the nature of IMF interactions with its member states has changed.[27] There are at least three changes that are relevant for current purposes:

1. *The political context within which the IMF must operate has changed.* Non-state actors – corporations, NGOs, civic organizations – have begun to play a greater role in international affairs generally and in the work of the IMF in particular. This can be seen, for example, in the consultation requirements in the PRSP process, the efforts the IMF makes to meet with civil society in its missions to its member states, and in its growing informal interactions with civil society over particular policy papers of the IMF. This evolving relationship has increased the pressure on the IMF to disclose more information and was an important factor in the establishment of the Independent Evaluation Office. NGOs and civic organizations, however, continue to criticize the IMF for the lack of transparency in its operating procedures. They argue that they do not fully understand how the IMF makes operational decisions and that it appears that its decision making process is subject to undue influence from the IMF's most powerful member states.
2. *The nature of the IMF's relations with its member states has changed.* Originally the IMF was perceived as and operated like a credit union in which all participants were both contributors to the fund and users of its services. Thus, all member states understood that IMF policy and operational decisions could become directly applicable to them. However, this is no longer the case. Today, the rich countries contribute most of the IMF's funds but never use its financial or technical services while the developing countries contribute a relatively small portion of its resources but use all its services. In addition, the rich countries, both because of the weighted voting structure in the IMF and the structure of its Executive Board, are able to control the institution and make operational policy for it, even though these policies will never be applicable to them or their citizens. The developing countries, who are dependent on the services of the IMF, on the other hand find it much more difficult to participate in policy and decision making of the IMF. The result of these changes is that a power

---

[26] R.H.R. Harper, *Inside the IMF: An Ethnography of Documents, Technology and Organizational Action* (1998) at 175-230 for a description of an IMF mission.

[27] See James M. Boughton, *Silent Revolution: The International Monetary Fund 1979-1989* (2001) for a history of the International Monetary Fund during much of this period.

imbalance has developed in the IMF.[28] In this situation, the lack of formal comprehensive operational policies and procedures becomes a problem that affects the perceived fairness of IMF operations and decision making.

3. *The scope of IMF operations has expanded dramatically.* The IMF, in addition to its involvement in monetary, fiscal and exchange rate policy, is now also involved in advising countries and in supporting their efforts to promote better governance, and to adopt policies that are geared towards poverty reduction as well as towards macroeconomic stability. The result is that a member state's central bank and ministry of finance do not have all the necessary information about the issues of interest to the IMF. Thus, the IMF needs to interact with a much broader array of governmental and non-governmental sources if it is to obtain the necessary information, and effectively design and implement its operations. All these sources can influence the success of its proposed activities. For these additional actors, the lack of clear and predictable IMF operating procedures becomes a problem because they do not know the most effective ways to engage with the IMF and cannot understand its operational needs.

The combined effect of these three changes is that the need for formal and comprehensive IMF operational procedures has become more urgent. The lack of such procedures is undermining the efficacy of the IMF and even threatening its legitimacy.

B. Situation in the World Bank[29]

The World Bank, unlike the IMF, has formal operational policies and procedures to guide its staff in the conduct of their responsibilities. Both of these are contained in the Bank's Operational Manual[30] which is available at the Bank's website. It addresses such issues as the types of products the Bank offers, the procedures Bank staff should follow in developing their country assistance strategies and other analytical work, the procedures they should follow and the factors they should consider in their project and loan preparatory work, the environmental and social safeguard policies of the Bank, the procedures applicable to loan disbursements and repayments and the staff's responsibilities in monitoring Bank-funded projects.

---

[28] See Daniel D. Bradlow (2001) 'Stuffing New Wine Into Old Bottles: The Troubling Case of the IMF', *Journal of International Banking Regulation*, **3**(1).

[29] The 'World Bank' refers to the members of the World Bank Group. The members of this group are the International Bank for Reconstruction and Development (IBRD), the International Development Association (IDA), the International Finance Corporation (IFC), the Multilateral Investment Guarantee Agency (MIGA) and the International Centre for Settlement of Investment Disputes.

[30] The Operations Manual can be viewed at www.worldbank.org/institutional/manuals/opmanual.nsf. This manual is only applicable to the IBRD and IDA. However, many of its policies and procedures have been incorporated into the operational policies and procedures of IFC and MIGA. See websites: www.ifc.org; www.miga.org.

The Bank's operational policies and procedures consist of a number of different documents. They are:[31]

1. *Operational Policies (OPs)*: These are short, focused statements that are drawn from the Bank's Articles of Agreement, the general conditions, and policies approved by the board. They establish the parameters within which Bank operations must be conducted and describe the circumstances under which exceptions to these policies are admissible and who can authorize such exceptions. In the terminology of this chapter, the OPs are the Bank's operational policies.
2. *Bank Procedures (BPs)*: These are statements explaining how Bank staff should implement the policies set out in the OPs. They spell out the procedures and documentation that staff are required to obtain. One of their purposes is to ensure Bank-wide consistency and quality in the implementation of the OPs. In the terminology of this chapter, the BPs are the Bank's operational procedures.
3. *Good Practices (GPs)*: They contain advice and guidance for staff on implementing the OPs. The GPs contain information on such matters as the history of the issue being addressed in the OP, the sectoral context within which the OP is being implemented, the analytical framework that has informed the substance of the OP, and they provide some best practice examples.
4. *Operational Directives (ODs)*: The ODs contain a mixture of policies, procedures and guidelines. They are gradually being replaced by OPs, BPs and GPs.
5. *Operational Memoranda (Op. Memos)*: These are interim instructions designed to elaborate on issues raised in OPs/BPs or ODs. Once the instructions in Op. Memos are incorporated into revisions of the pertinent OPs/BPs, the Op. Memos are retired.

OPs, BPs and ODs, which are contained in the Operational Manual, are mandatory and the staff is expected to comply with their terms in all operational activity. GPs and Op. Memos are not mandatory and may not be in the Operational Manual.

The Bank has established a number of independent mechanisms for monitoring and ensuring staff compliance with these operational policies and procedures.[32] They are:

---

[31] These descriptions are drawn from the definitions of these documents contained in the Operations Manual, *idem.*

[32] In the case of the IBRD and IDA these independent mechanisms are in addition to the Operations Policy and Country Services Vice Presidency, which is responsible for strengthening management systems for monitoring compliance. See World Bank, *Quality Assurance Group*, available at http://web.worldbank.org/WBSITE/EXTERNAL/PROJECTS/QAG/0,,pagePK:109619~theSitePK:109609,00.html.

1. *Operations Evaluation Department (OED)*:[33] The OED is responsible for evaluating completed Bank projects and for offering the management insights into the strengths and weaknesses in Bank operations. Its activities may lead it to recommend changes in Bank operating policies and procedures.
2. *Inspection Panel (Panel)*:[34] The Panel, whose jurisdiction is limited to IBRD and IDA operations, is authorized to receive requests from any groups of two or more persons who claim that they have been or are threatened with harm by the Bank's failure to act in compliance with its operational policies and procedures. The Panel is authorized to investigate these complaints and make recommendations to the Bank's Executive Board on how to correct the problems caused by Bank non-compliance with these policies and procedures.
3. *The Compliance Advisor Ombudsman (CAO)*:[35] The CAO's jurisdiction is limited to the social and environmental aspects of IFC and MIGA operations. It is authorized to deal with complaints received from persons who claim they have been or are threatened with harm caused by IFC or MIGA funded operations, to monitor compliance with IFC and MIGA social and environmental standards and operational procedures and to give the management of these institutions advice on the social and environmental aspect of its operations.

The Bank's personnel policies and procedures have a similar structure to the IMF. It has a staff manual that informs staff about their rights and responsibilities. In addition, the Bank, like the IMF, has an Administrative Tribunal, an Ombudsman, and an Ethics Officer. Their powers and procedures are similar to those of the corresponding bodies in the IMF.

Situation in Regional Development Banks[36]

The African, Asian and Inter-American Development Banks and the European Bank for Reconstruction and Development follow similar approaches to the World Bank. This means that they each have operational policies and procedures to guide their staff in the conduct of their operations. All four have an evaluation department that helps monitor the implementation of these operational policies and

---

[33] World Bank, *Operations Evaluation Department*, www.worldbank.org/oed/.

[34] World Bank, *The Inspection Panel*, available at http://wbln0018.worldbank.org/ipn/ipnweb.nsf.

[35] *Compliance Advisor Ombudsman*, www.cao-ombudsman.org/ev.php.

[36] For information on the operational policies and procedures of these banks, see www.iadb.org/exr/english/POLICIES/policies.htm for the Inter-American Development Bank; see www.adb.org/Development/policies.asp and www.adb.org/Documents/Manuals/Operations/default.asp?p=policies for the Asian Development Bank; see www.afdb.org/projects/policies_and_procedures.htm?n1=3&n2=1&n3=0 for the African Development Bank; see www.ebrd.org/about/index.htm for the European Bank for Reconstruction and Development.

procedures. In addition, the Asian, and Inter-American Development Banks and the European Bank for Reconstruction and Development have inspection mechanisms to monitor compliance with these policies and procedures and to deal with the harm that they cause.[37] Finally, each of the regional development banks has personnel policies and mechanisms for dealing with grievances that may arise under them.

Designing a Formal and Comprehensive Set of Operational Policies and Procedures for the IMF

The previous section makes it clear that the IMF is an unusual international financial institution (IFI) because it does not have a set of formal and comprehensive operational policies and procedures. There are two possible explanations for this difference. The first is that the IMF's lack of such procedures is attributable to the significant operational differences that follow from the macroeconomic focus of the IMF's responsibilities compared to the MDBs' emphasis on project lending. However, this is not an adequate justification for the IMF's lack of a formal set of operational procedures. The scope of the IMF's interactions in those member states that use its services tends to be no less diverse or complex than the interactions of the MDBs in these societies. In addition, the impact of an IMF operation on a particular state tends to be stronger than the impact of most MDB operations on the same state. Consequently, it has the same need for transparent and predictable procedures to guide the conduct of staff and management as the MDBs.

The second possible explanation is that the costs to the IMF of having formal operational procedures are too high. In order to adequately assess this explanation, it is necessary to determine both the costs and benefits that such procedures would create for the IMF.

A. The Benefits

There are five significant benefits that would accrue to the IMF from having a set of formal operational procedures. They are:

1. *Effective Guidance for Staff*: Formal operational procedures would provide staff and management with a clearer understanding of what is expected from them during IMF operations. This should facilitate staff accountability and provide a basis for improving staff performance. It should also facilitate the decentralization of IMF operational decision making, which may help promote member state 'ownership' of IMF-

[37] Asian Development Bank, *Inspection Function*, www.adb.org/Inspection/default.asp; European Bank for Reconstruction and Development, *Independent Recourse Mechanism*, www.ebrd.org/about/policies/irm/irm.pdf. The Inter-American Development Bank does not mention its Investigation Review Mechanism on its website.

funded programs. Finally, these procedures may positively affect staff willingness to be innovative by giving them clear guidance on where there is scope for innovation.

2. *Predictability in the Conduct of IMF Operations*: Formal operational procedures provide greater predictability to IMF operations than informal procedures which can relatively easily be changed. This will enhance both stakeholder confidence in dealing with the IMF and IMF staff confidence in their interactions with outside stakeholders.
3. *Transparency in IMF Decision Making and Action*: Formal procedures would make it easier for outsiders to understand how the IMF does its work and the factors that it considers in making its decisions. This should help clarify the scope of IMF responsibilities and differentiate them from the responsibilities of member governments in their dealings with the IMF. Increased transparency may also reduce suspicion that the IMF management is unaccountable, has too much discretion and is susceptible to pressure from powerful member states in its decision making.
4. *Accountability*: Formal operational procedures will promote accountability in two ways. First, they will give outside stakeholders – member states and non-state actors – a principled basis on which to hold IMF staff and management accountable. This should help depoliticize the issue of IMF operational accountability for specific operations and decisions. Second, formal procedures will help the board members to hold IMF staff and management accountable.
5. *Lessons Learned*: Formal operational procedures will also make it easier for the IMF to learn about the actual impact of its operational practices and the strengths and weaknesses of its operational policies and procedures and to improve them over time.

B. The Costs

The IMF would incur the following costs from having formal operational procedures:

1. *Increased Bureaucratization*: Formal operational procedures can result in IMF staff developing a cautious approach to their work in which they seek to do everything 'by the book'. There is also a danger that the rules result in an increase in reporting and paperwork requirements that reduce staff productivity.
2. *Loss of Flexibility*: It is impossible for the drafters of the procedures to anticipate all the situations in which they need to be applied. Thus, the procedures can result in a certain loss of operational flexibility because they cannot be easily adapted to specific conditions in which they actually must function. This in turn may cause the IMF, once again, to be seen as imposing a 'one size fits all' approach on its member states.
3. *Disincentives for Innovation*: Formal procedures can increase the risk that staff and management will be sanctioned for being innovative in ways that

do not strictly comply with strict interpretations of the procedures. Since the issues with which the IMF deals do not have clear answers and their resolution requires creativity, any disincentive to innovation is a potentially significant cost for the IMF. The cost however is mitigated by the fact that it is not in the IMF's interest for the staff and management to have too much scope for uncontrolled innovation and the procedures can establish the limits on their scope for permissible ingenuity.

C. Balancing Costs and Benefits

There are four reasons why the benefits of having formal operational policies and procedures outweigh the costs for the IMF. First, such procedures help outside stakeholders engage effectively with the IMF, which is particularly relevant at a time when the IMF is advocating increased participation in the PRSP process, increased country ownership of IMF-supported programs and transparency, participation and accountability as key elements in good governance for its member states. Second, transparent and predictable operational procedures will increase public understanding of the IMF's operations, including of the costs associated with more transparent operating procedures. Third, the procedures will promote IMF accountability. Fourth, the policies and procedures will improve internal IMF governance at a time when IMF operations are growing more complex. All these benefits would be earned in areas where the IMF is particularly weak: public confidence and trust in the IMF and the efficacy of its operations is declining and there is a growing mismatch between the IMF's rhetoric on good governance and its own governance practices.

Given these significant gains, the question of whether or not the IMF should adopt a set of formal operational rules and procedures seems to boil down to two questions:

1. Can the IMF draft operational policies and procedures that maximise the benefits while minimising the costs associated with such policies and procedures?
2. What should the scope of the policies and procedures be?

Each of these questions is answered below.

C.1: Drafting Operational Policies and Procedures

The primary drafting challenge is to strike the appropriate balance between the rigidity needed to provide stakeholders with the desired predictability and transparency in IMF operations and the flexibility needed for management and staff to adapt the policies and procedures to the variety of situations in which they must operate. There is no theoretical reason that this cannot be done. In fact, it is the type of drafting challenge that government drafts-people confront all the time.

In this case the goal is to draft operational policies that are sufficiently detailed that they provide all stakeholders with the predictability and information that they need to understand the policies of the IMF and their operational goals when they implement the policies. The objective in drafting the operational procedures is to identify the categories of information staff need to gather in order to perform their operational responsibilities; the factors they should consider, the people they should consult and the steps they should follow in making operational decisions. In addition, the procedures should clearly explain how staff can seek exceptions to the policies and procedures. There are two good models that the IMF could use in this drafting exercise. The first is the IMF's own *New Conditionality Guidelines* and its *Operational Guidance on the New Conditionality Guidelines.*[38] The second is the Bank's three related operational documents – OPs, BPs and GPs. These examples clearly demonstrate that it is possible for the IMF to develop operational policies and procedures that combine predictability and transparency in IMF operations with operational flexibility.

C.2: The Scope of the Operational Rules and Procedures

There are two aspects to this issue. First, the operational policies and procedures should address how the IMF conducts its operations and makes decisions relating to all aspects of its work. This means that they should cover all aspects of IMF surveillance, the design, negotiation and implementation of IMF financial programs, IMF technical assistance, policy and analytical work and its relations with other organizations.

Second, the IMF needs to establish a transparent and predictable rule-making procedure that will govern how the IMF develops all its operational policies and procedures. The extensive consultation that preceded the adoption of the current guidelines on conditionality and of the work plan of the Independent Evaluation Office are important precedents in this regard. However, in each of these cases this impressive process was 'revealed' to all interested parties as it unfolded. Instead, the IMF needs to establish a predictable rule-making procedure that it will always follow when developing new operational policies and procedures. This is consistent with general principles of good governance that the IMF advocates to its member states.

The Need for an Ombudsman in the IMF

In order for operational policies and procedures to be effective, they need to be supported by a mechanism capable of monitoring and promoting compliance with them. One indication of the importance of such mechanisms is that the MDBs either have or are considering establishing an inspection mechanism that is empowered to investigate charges of non-compliance with their operational policies and procedures.[39]

---

[38] *Guidelines on Conditionality, supra* note 3, *Operational Guidance on the New Conditionality Guidelines*, *supra* note 5.

[39] See World Bank, *The Inspection Panel*, http://wbln0018.worldbank.org/ipn/ipnweb.nsf; International Finance Corporation (IFC)-Multilateral Investment Guarantee Agency (MIGA), *Office of Compliance Advisor/Ombudsman*, www.cao-ombudsman.org/ev.php;

There are a number of benefits that such mechanisms offer to IFIs. First, the mechanisms can help raise the profile of the operational policies and procedures within the institution. In this regard the experience of the World Bank's Inspection Panel is instructive. The risk that Bank projects may become the object of Panel investigations has increased staff sensitivity to the Bank's operational policies and procedures and their interest in acting in compliance with them. In fact, it has led to a phenomenon known as 'Panel-proofing' a project, which means making sure that the project is sufficiently in compliance with the policies and procedures that it will survive any challenge in the Inspection Panel.

Second, the mechanism can become a vehicle for solving problems that have arisen in IFI operations. Such problem-solving capability offers obvious advantages in terms of the quality of the operations of the institution and in terms of public relations. The IFC and MIGA's Compliance Advisor Ombudsman (CAO) offers the best example of an effective problem-solving mechanism.

Third, the mechanism offers the institution an opportunity for learning lessons about the actual impact of its operations. Since these mechanisms are triggered by complaints from those who have been most directly affected by the operation, they have a unique perspective on the operations of the institution. Consequently, its findings and the expertise it develops over time can offer the institution some important insights into the strengths and weaknesses of its operations and into what feasible improvements can be made to both the policies with which its operations must comply and the procedures that it should follow in designing and implementing these operations.

Fourth, the mechanism is helpful in differentiating the responsibilities of the international financial institution from those of other actors in its operations. This is a particularly useful benefit for an institution like the IMF which has to be careful to avoid unduly interfering with the sovereignty of its member states. The mechanism, whose mandate is limited to monitoring issues arising under the institution's operational policies and procedures, can focus just on the operations of the institution without having to investigate the activities and decisions of its member states. The evolution in the functioning of the World Bank's Inspection Panel shows both the sensitivity and importance of this issue and the ability of such mechanisms to enhance institutional accountability without unduly interfering with the sovereignty of its member states.[40]

The above suggests that the efficacy of the IMF's operational policies and procedures would be enhanced if it established a mechanism that was empowered

---

Asian Development Bank, *Inspection Function*, www.adb.org/Inspection/default.asp; European Bank for Reconstruction and Development, *Independent Recourse Mechanism*, www.ebrd.org/about/policies/irm/irm.pdf, Inter-American Development Bank, *Independent Investigation Mechanism*, www.iadb.org/cont/poli/mecanism.pdf; The African Development Bank is also being encouraged by the G-7 to establish such a mechanism.

[40] See Ibrahim F.I. Shihata, *The World Bank Inspection Panel: In Practice* (2d ed. 2000); Daniel D. Bradlow (2001) 'Lessons From the NGO Campaign Against the Second Review of the World Bank Inspection Panel: A Participant's Perspective', *Journal of International and Comparative Law*, **7**.

to monitor their implementation. There are a number of forms such a mechanism could take. For example, the IMF could follow the examples of the IBRD and IDA, and the regional development banks and establish an inspection mechanism.[41] Alternatively, it could follow the example of the IFC and MIGA and establish a compliance advisor and ombudsman arrangement. A third possibility is to follow the example of many national governments and the European Union and appoint an ombudsman.[42]

Based on the experience of all these examples, it is possible to deduce certain general principles that should be observed by any IFI interested in establishing a mechanism to monitor the implementation of its operational policies and procedures. Any mechanism that fails to incorporate these principles is likely to be viewed as deficient by at least one of the IFI's stakeholders.

These principles are:

1. *Role of Non-State Actors*: It is absolutely essential that the mechanism be triggered by complaints received from non-state actors who claim that they have been harmed or threatened with harm by the failure of the IMF to comply with its operational rules and procedures.
2. *Clarity of Purpose*: The mechanism can be designed to serve one or more of three different functions. These functions are:
    a. Compliance Review: This involves determining if the IFI staff and management are satisfying the requirements of all the applicable operating policies and procedures in a particular IFI operation. The World Bank's Inspection Panel is a good example of an inspection mechanism whose primary focus is compliance review.
    b. Problem Solving: This involves resolving problems that arise in the course of an IMF operation and that have been identified by affected people as causing them or threatening them with harm. The IFC and MIGA's CAO is a good example of a problem-solving mechanism.
    c. Lessons Learned: This refers to the ability of the mechanism to contribute to the lessons that the IMF can learn about the efficacy of its operational rules and procedures. Given its unique perspective, the mechanism is in a position to identify trends within the implementation of operational policies and procedures that are unlikely to be obvious to other IFI actors. This function is not well developed in most of the mechanisms in the MDBs. The European Union's ombudsman is an example of a mechanism that performs a 'lessons learned' role.

    These three purposes are not necessarily mutually exclusive and it is possible for one inspection mechanism to perform more than one of these functions. In the case of the IMF, the two most relevant functions will be

---

[41] See, *supra*, note 40. The United Nations also has an inspection mechanism, although this is not triggered by outside complaints. See, United Nations, *Joint Inspection Unit (JIU)*, www.unsystem.org/jiu/.

[42] European Ombudsman, www.euro-ombudsman.eu.int/home/en/default.htm.

the compliance review and lessons learned function. It is more difficult for the mechanism to perform a problem solving function because of the complexities and multi-faceted nature of IMF operations. However, this does not mean that it should not be given the ability to solve problems when it can appropriately do so.

3. *Limited Jurisdiction*: The mechanism's jurisdiction must be limited to any case arising out of an allegation of non-compliance by the IFI staff and management with the IFI's operational policies and procedures. This helps ensure that the mechanism does not encroach onto the sovereignty of the institution's member states.

4. *User Friendliness*: Since the mechanism is intended to be available to those who have been adversely affected by the operations of the IFI, its procedures for receiving and handling complaints should be as easy for the affected people to understand and utilise as possible. One way to make the mechanism user friendly is to limit the number of requirements that a complaint must satisfy before the mechanism begins to address the substance of the matters raised in the complaint. The Ombudsman part of the CAO is a good example of a user friendly mechanism. An example of a mechanism that is not particularly user friendly is the World Bank Inspection Panel.[43] One consequence of its formal procedures is that the management of the World Bank has been able to use the Panel procedures to challenge the eligibility of complainants and the suitability of complaints for investigation. This has forced affected people to rely on relatively sophisticated advisors in preparing their complaints. In some cases, it has also contributed to an unnecessary politicization of the complaint.

5. *Independence*: The mechanism should be independent of the management of the IMF and should report directly to its Executive Board. In addition, the terms and conditions of employment of the mechanism's personnel should be designed to promote and protect its independence. Finally, the budget of the mechanism should support its independence.

6. *Powers of Investigation*: The mechanism must have access to all the persons, documents, records, and locations that it deems necessary to conduct a complete investigation.

7. *Impartiality and Competence*: This means that the mechanism's recommendations, findings and conclusions must be supported by facts and well-reasoned arguments. In addition, the mechanism's investigations should be sufficiently comprehensive to demonstrate that it has gathered all the relevant information and has used this information in its reports.

8. *Efficiency and Cost Effectiveness*: This means the mechanism should be able to deal with complaints relatively quickly and at a cost that does not impose an undue burden on the IMF.

[43] See, *supra*, note 40.

9. *Effective Management of Issues Presented*: This means that the mechanism must be able to demonstrate to all stakeholders that its findings and recommendations are taken seriously by the IFI and that the IFI will either implement the mechanism's recommendations or explain its failure to do so. One important consequence of this principle is that the mechanism should be given the power to monitor the implementation of the results of an inspection process.
10. *Transparency*: This means that the mechanism must publish the results of its investigations and must publish an annual report.

Application of the Principles to the IMF

Given the complexity of the IMF's operations, it needs a mechanism that is flexible, efficient, effective and easy to use. It also needs a mechanism that can both monitor staff and management compliance with its operational policies and procedures and can provide the IMF with a lessons learned capability. The mechanism should also, where appropriate, be able to help those directly affected by the IMF's decisions and operations either resolve their problems with the staff and management, or explain to them why a resolution is not possible.

The model that is most suited to the IMF's needs is an ombudsman. Historically an ombudsman was created for the purpose of receiving complaints from people who believed that they had been harmed by the failure of an institution to comply with its own policies and procedures.[44] It was also expected to report to higher authorities on how well the institution was performing its responsibilities and complying with its policies and procedures. An ombudsman was designed to be flexible and relatively informal in its approach to the issues brought to it. This means that it can perform its function with minimal procedural requirements. The ombudsman is also well suited to help educate the institution and the authorities to which it reports on the problems that are arising in its operations and on identifying ways in which it can improve its operations.

The following are the essential characteristics that should be exhibited by an IMF ombudsman charged with monitoring its operational policies and procedures:

1. The ombudsman must be appointed by and report directly to the IMF's Executive Board. He/she should have the status of a senior official of the IMF.
2. The ombudsman must be given all the indicia of independence. This means he/she should not have to report to IMF management or to receive any authorization from management regarding its budget or personnel decisions. He/she must be appointed to a single non-renewable term of office from which he/she can only be removed by the Executive Board for

[44] For information on ombudsmen generally, see Ibrahim al-Wahab, *The Swedish Institution of Ombudsman* (1979); World Bank, PREM Notes, No. 19, April 1999, *Using an Ombudsman to Oversee Public Officials*, www1.worldbank.org/prem/PREMNotes/premnote19.pdf.

cause. The ombudsman should also have full control over all staff appointments in the ombudsman's office, and assured budgetary support.

3. The ombudsman must be able to receive any complaint relating to the IMF's operations from any person who believes they have been or are threatened with harm caused by the failure of IMF staff or management to comply with the IMF's operational policies and procedures.
4. The ombudsman must have the exclusive power to review the complaint and to decide whether to investigate the complaint or to reject it.
5. If the ombudsman decides to accept the complaint for investigation, he/she must have complete powers of investigation, which includes access to all the IMF staff and records that he/she deems relevant to the investigation.
6. The ombudsman must be required to make a report, which is publicly available, to the Executive Board for each case for which he/she conducts a full investigation.
7. The ombudsman must publish an annual report in which he/she must report on all the complaints he/she received and on how they were handled. In addition, the ombudsman, in the annual report, must comment on the lessons he/she believes can be learned about the IMF's operational policies and procedures from the cases he/she has received and, if appropriate, make suggestions on how to improve these rules and procedures.
8. The ombudsman must have the authority to monitor the implementation of the outcome of any investigations he/she conducts.

Conclusion

The complexity and range of IMF operations has grown to the point where it is no longer feasible for it to limit its interactions in its member states to officials in the central bank and the ministry of finance in those countries. It now regularly consults with a broad range of government officials, legislatures and actors in civil society in those member states that utilise its services. This means that the number and range of actors with which the IMF is engaged has grown beyond the point where its operating practices can be kept informal and known only to a relatively small number of experts. Consequently, it needs to develop a set of operational policies and procedures to guide its interactions with all these actors and to guide its decision making. The lack of a comprehensive set of such policies and procedures renders IMF operations unduly opaque and undermines stakeholder confidence in its fairness and impartiality.

While the creation of such operational policies and procedures does impose some costs on the IMF, they can be minimised through the policy and procedures design and drafting process. In addition, these costs are more than compensated for by the benefits that they will bring to the institution.

It is not sufficient for the IMF to merely promulgate such policies and procedures. It must support the implementation of these operational policies and procedures by establishing an independent ombudsman with the authority to investigate complaints from directly affected people and groups about staff and management non-compliance with the policies and procedures.

Both of these steps are required if the IMF is to demonstrate that it practises what it preaches about good governance.

Note 3

Tighter IMF Accountability? Some Dangers

Robert Hunter Wade[45]

Professor Bradlow's argument seems to be as self-evidently true as motherhood and apple pie. Of course it would be a good thing if the IMF had more 'formal and comprehensive' operational policies and procedures, more public disclosure of what it is doing, and an ombudsman able to investigate complaints from non-state actors who claim that they have been harmed or threatened with harm by the failure of the IMF to comply with those operational policies and procedures. More accountability is always better. Or is it? A little 'ground truthing' is in order.

There are some immediate objections to Bradlow's proposals, and some deeper problems. The immediate ones include the point that the Fund already has plenty of 'formal and comprehensive' operational policies and procedures, laid out on the Fund's website and in public documents. By what criteria are more needed? Moreover, the Fund has recently established an Independent Evaluation Office (IEO) that is carrying out part of the role of an ombudsman; and it is seeking public comment on its work. Should one not wait to see what impact the IEO is making before setting up a new inspection regime?

Now, to the deeper issues: is Bradlow's an appropriate model of accountability for the Fund (as distinct from the Bank)? To whom would the Fund end up being more accountable? Who gets to set the appropriate standards, policies and procedures, and which nation's political culture would inform their content? How to establish the ombudsman function so that it is captured neither by management nor by Fund critics, and avoids creating the risk-averse behaviour that the Bank's Inspection Panel has prompted inside the Bank?

The core of the argument is this: increased accountability of an organization is not necessarily a good thing; it also depends on accountability to whom. In the case of the IMF (like the World Bank), the concentration of structural power in the hands of 'developed', creditor countries means that more accountability translates as more accountability to the developed, creditor countries, not to the 'developing', borrower countries. Institutionalizing more accountability is a way of undercutting the demands from the developing countries

---

45 Professor of Political Economy, London School of Economics; author of 'Greening the Bank. The Struggle Over the Environment, 1970-1995', in D. Kapur, J. Lewis, R. Webb (eds.), *The World Bank: Its First Half Century*, vol. 2, Washington DC: Brookings.

for an increased role in the governance of the organizations, and reining in any expansion of the organizations' autonomy – autonomy from the preferences of the Northern member states, something the Northern states are determined to prevent. Since the Northern member states know that they will never depend on either the Fund or the Bank, their dominance gives them scope for opportunism and carelessness in the conditions they require others to meet. The accountability mechanisms being proposed do not begin to address this problem.

Inapplicability of Bradlow's Accountability Model

Bradlow was a key architect of the World Bank's Inspection Panel, and his argument for the Fund applies much the same underlying model of accountability. But it is not clear that a model designed for a project-based organization is appropriate for a program-based organization. Fund programs have macroeconomic targets and conditions, and it would be hard to ascribe specific harm from the general provisions of Fund programs – which is feasible, in principle, in the case of projects that affect a specific set of people (the people to be moved from a coming reservoir, for example). Then there is the 'agency' problem in the form of the slippage between the Fund's program intentions and the specific steps taken by the national government to implement them; which again complicates the judgement of Fund accountability.

The Problem of Asymmetrical Accountability

The Fund should be more accountable to whom? The organization is in effect run by a condominium of a small group of states, ranging in number from one (G-1), the United States, to seven (G-7). They set the rules and decide what the Fund will do in crises, such as the Asian crisis of 1997-98. On the other hand, the Fund's clients are the developing countries, which operate primarily in the status of petitioners for loans and easy conditions.

In the present power structure, it is difficult to see how proposals for more accountability would not mean, in effect, more accountable to the US above all (the US Treasury, Congress, and US-based NGOs). This might erode rather than strengthen the Fund's legitimacy, at least in the developing world. It is going to be a long time before the US and the rest of the G-7 are willing to dilute their dominance and give more influence to representatives of states who know that their own state might someday have to follow the rules they are setting for others.

When some developing country representatives began to press the issue of increasing the voting share of developing countries in the boards of the Bank and the Fund in 2003, the response of the US Executive Director was sharp. 'We reject the proposal to increase the number of basic votes ... The increase in developing countries' share of votes ... would not be material [because of the informal custom of making decisions on a consensus basis ...], would do more harm than good and, in our view, would be inconsistent with the principle that country shares in the IFIs

[International Financial Institutions] should reflect relative economic weights in the world economy ... Giving population and other factors a weight in voting strength would create a radically different, less desirable and non-financial structure for the Bank'.[46]

In practice, more Fund accountability would translate into more accountability to Western NGO watchdogs (as well as G-7 governments). This raises the separate question of how to make the exploding sector of watchdog NGOs more accountable. Some do not disclose their financing, or set policy through some explicit process of debating the views of members, or have members at all, and their claim to be acting in the best interest of those for whom they claim to speak rests on uncertain foundations. In American political culture it is a matter for outrage when important decisions are made in a way that excludes any affected interest group, and the fragmentation of public power provides ample access points through which even small NGOs with a foundation grant and catchy name can claim a voice. Hence all the attention is on the accountability of public entities, not on that of the watchdogs whose virtue is taken for granted.

Who Sets the Content of the 'Formal and Comprehensive' Operational Policies and Procedures, and What Incentive Do They Have to Recognise Varying Capacities and Preferences Among the Borrower States?

Bradlow emphasises the need for explicit rule-making procedures so that insiders and outsiders know exactly how its policies and procedures are developed. Making the procedures explicit and public will benefit especially the weaker member states, he implies, which become less subject to the covertly-pressed self-interested demands of the stronger. Perhaps; but in the present power structures the content of the additional policies and procedures may only serve to strengthen the dominance of the G-7.

The existing asymmetry of power creates what could be called a 'moral hazard' problem in Fund governance (and equally in World Bank governance).[47] 'Moral hazard' handicaps the Fund's ability to advance a common good whose characteristics are defined by debate between state representatives on the Fund's board of directors. First, the G-7 set standards for others knowing they will not have to meet the same standards. Second, the G-7 often insist that the Fund require developing countries to act in ways that clearly advance G-7 interests but less clearly advance the developing countries' interests.[48]

---

[46] Carole Brookins, 'Enhancing the Voice of Developing and Transition Countries at the World Bank', EDS2003-0389, Office of the US Executive Director, World Bank, 20 June 2003.

[47] 'Moral hazard' comes from the economics of insurance, where it refers to the tendency of insurance to generate carelessness. I use the term in an extended sense.

[48] For a case study of malign Fund pressure on Ethiopia to open its capital account – strongly backed by the US Treasury – see Wade, 'Capital and Revenge: the IMF and Ethiopia', *Challenge*, September/October 2001, pp. 67-75. Much of the Fund's intervention

For example, the G-7 are likely to set rules and requirements that err on the side of 'international best practice', making no allowance for the range of state capacities that the Fund has to deal with. This then opens up unlimited opportunities for critics of the Fund (think US Congress) and of a particular Fund member (think China), to attack the Fund and indirectly the member government for failure to comply, while overlooking similar lapses on the part of states that are important for US strategic objectives at the time (think Turkey, Iraq, Afghanistan, Pakistan, Jordan).

This, at any rate, has been the case in the World Bank. Consider the Bank's Qinghai project, prepared in the mid to late 1990s.[49] The Qinghai project became the subject of an 'NGO swarm' in 1999–2000, and the swarm was successful in getting the Bank to withdraw from the project (formally, in getting the Chinese government to withdraw it from the Bank).

Qinghai province is about the poorest in China, and its provincial administration had never done a World Bank project before. The project consisted of a small irrigation dam and canal, and voluntary settlement on new irrigation farms of some 60,000 dirt-poor people from the eastern part of the same province. The provincial administration was determined to do the environmental assessment largely with its own staff guided by a World Bank consultant. The US NGOs which led the campaign against the project attacked the environmental assessment as third rate, ignoring the point about local learning and also ignoring that no one was able to point to serious environmental dangers likely to be realized if the project went ahead. (Not even the very critical Inspection Panel Report could point to likely serious dangers, as distinct from procedural flaws in the environmental assessment.)

The NGO critics – boosted by Congressional members delighted to use the opportunity to bash the Bank, foreign aid, and China all at the same time – took for granted that an environmental assessment, anywhere, had to be done to 'international standards' as defined by the (Western) international community of environmental assessors. They ignored the difference between China, trying to ensure that these skills are domesticated, and Indonesia, which has produced world-class environmental assessments for many Bank projects over many years and still has hardly a single citizen able to do an environmental assessment unaided by foreign experts because the ones for the Bank were done by flown-in consultants.

---

in the East Asian crisis of 1997-98 is open to the same interpretation. See Paul Blustein (2001) *The Chastening: Inside The Crisis That Rocked the Global Financial System and Humbled the IMF*, Public Affairs Books, New York.

[49] The Qinghai project was in Qinghai province (next to Tibet), and it formed one of three provincial components of the China Western Poverty Reduction Project. My remarks about the Qinghai investigation by the Bank's Inspection Panel are based on work as a consultant to the Panel in the Qinghai investigation, from October to December 1999, and on following the case subsequently to the Chinese government's withdrawal of it from the Bank in July 2000. My task was to write a report to the Panel about how the project had been prepared inside the Bank. I came to very different conclusions about the Bank's role in the project to those reached by the Panel.

Those who press for tighter IMF accountability, then, have to address the question of how to ensure that the formal and comprehensive operational policies and procedures adopted by the Fund are indeed flexible enough to avoid providing an almost guaranteed margin of non-compliance for NGO and US Congressional critics to mount campaigns against the Fund, and make it ever more responsive to the preferences of the US government.

As another illustration of the problem of asymmetrical accountability, consider the case of the Fund's conditions on its loans. The number of conditions multiplied from an average of around eight 'performance criteria' per loan during the 1980s to some 26 during the 1990s.[50] Of course, the Fund's staff and management are aware that the multiplication of conditions on loans can have diminishing returns and undermine the effectiveness of conditionality. The recent *Guidelines on Conditionality* call for streamlining the conditions to those essential to the program; and there has indeed been some reduction latterly. But the watchdogs tend to want more conditions, seeing them as protection against the waste of taxpayers' money. Which NGOs, which Congressional bodies, are going to complain about the Fund's failure to comply with its own streamlining guidelines? The recent stand-by arrangement with Turkey had about 100 structural benchmarks and conditions.

How to Ensure the Independence and Legitimacy of the Ombudsman?

The ombudsman has to be seen to be independent from the board and the management – and also from NGO and Congressional watchdogs. This raises difficult issues of organisational design.

Consider the World Bank's 'independent' Inspection Panel.[51] Its existence and mandate has been the most persistently divisive issue on the board of the Bank since its creation in 1993, with the US and a few other non-borrower countries strongly in favour and virtually all developing countries against. The Panel's creation owes everything to US NGOs and the US Congress (though Bradlow and some other academic lawyers had key roles in formulating the idea).

The Panel has accordingly been highly responsive to the preferences of NGOs, because they are its main support base. It needs to score 'knock outs' from time to time to keep them on side. On the other hand, the Bank's board has for the most part taken a lackadaisical attitude to the question of who the President

[50] Devesh Kapur (2001) 'Expansive Agendas and Weak Instruments: Governance Related Conditionalities of the International Financial Institutions', *Journal of Policy Reform* **4**(3); Ngaire Woods (2002) 'Global Governance and the Role of Institutions', in *Governing Globalization: Power, Authority and Global Governance*, eds. David Held and Andrew McGrew, Cambridge: Polity.

[51] For background on the World Bank's Inspection Panel and an assessment of its effectiveness see Jonathan Fox, 'The World Bank Inspection Panel and the Limits of Accountability', in Jonathan Pincus and Jeffrey Winters (eds.) (2002) *Reinventing the World Bank*, Ithaca: Cornell University Press.

nominates as Panel members (the board is meant to have a co-equal role in the selection). The President, needing to keep enough NGOs inside the tent, is responsive to the personnel preferences of NGOs.

No surprise then that for much of its history the Panel has had a predominance of members who are out 'to get the Bank'. It has operated 'Star Chamber' procedures of interrogation of Bank staff. There has developed a syndrome of mistrust between it and Bank staff – a syndrome in the sense that the behaviour of each side merely confirms the negative expectations of the other. In particular, Bank staff respond to the threat of the Panel by becoming highly risk-averse, avoiding projects of the kind that might attract an investigation, and tying the Bank up in endless paperwork responding to the Panel's enquiries. This response has raised questions in the eyes of borrower governments about the Bank's overall benefit to them.

Bradlow recommends for the Fund an ombudsman, not an inspection panel. One of the important differences is that the Bank's Panel is formally limited largely to the function of 'compliance review', reflecting the hostility of the developing country Executive Directors to its very existence. The Fund's ombudsman, in Bradlow's proposal, would also be permitted to engage in 'problem solving' and in 'learning lessons'. This may well soften the pressures for it to become, like the Inspection Panel, prosecutor, judge and jury all in one.

However the danger remains – even with an ombudsman rather than an inspection panel – of a syndrome of mistrust developing between ombudsman and IMF staff. This is because the Fund and the ombudsman operate within the mistrust-hardening assumptions of American political culture.

The culture assumes, first, antagonistic relations between regulators and regulatees. It assumes, second, a punishment-based notion of accountability, such that 'no punishment, no accountability'. This is much more of an American notion of accountability than a European or Japanese one, and the American NGOs who shape the thinking of the Bank's Inspection Panel take it as obviously true that non-compliance implies that someone is to blame. Panel members have in the past pointed to specific Bank staff as culpable (in informal discussions with NGOs and management, though not in Panel reports), and supported NGO leaders in their lobbying of senior management to have those staff members punished. Not surprisingly the panellists limit their pointing to lower-level operational staff, never to senior management, as though the foot-soldiers are to be blamed for fighting wars.

The third assumption of US political culture is 'multilateralism at our convenience', meaning 'we will cooperate with other nations in multilateral organizations provided they do what we want'.

This multilateralism of convenience plus the other two assumptions were all on display in the behaviour of the US Congress after the board of the Bank voted to allow the Qinghai component to be put on hold while the Inspection Panel did an investigation, against the demand of the US that the Bank withdraw immediately. In high indignation the Senate voted to cut the US appropriation for IDA (the Bank's soft loan fund) from US$803 million to US$785 million; the House voted to cut the contribution to US$576. Representative Christopher Cox presented a bill which among many other punitive clauses required automatic cuts in US payments to IDA 'if the institution has not developed and implemented a 'pay-for-performance policy' which requires salary or pay reduction, or termination of employment, for any employee of the institution who is involved in the preparation, appraisal, or implementation of any project or activity which, if conducted, would violate any environmental or social policy of the World Bank group'.[52] The bill was not passed, but it illustrates the spirit towards multilateral organizations prevalent in the US legislature. No other legislature in the world presumes that it is entitled to dictate what a multilateral organization does.

The danger, then, is that the US's dominance of the Fund – and the assumptions it brings to that dominance – would push the ombudsman to interact with the Fund in a way that generates a syndrome of mistrust, as has happened in the Bank, resulting in more paperwork, more caution, and less flexibility in the relation of the Fund with members.

On the other hand, more public disclosure of what the Fund has required of a borrower, and the justification, would surely be a good thing. It might check the kind of abuse of Fund authority shown in the Fund's dealings with Ethiopia, referred to earlier. If the Fund had had to justify openly why it was refusing to extend Ethiopia's eligibility for the Extended Structural Adjustment Program (and hence for cheaper Fund credits) until the government agreed to open the capital account, even though Ethiopia had met the other conditions, it probably would not have been so silly. More open disclosure of the reasons for the terms and conditions of Fund loans to specific borrowers, combined with an institutional commitment on the part of managers to learn from the evaluations of the Independent Evaluation Office, may together address one of the Fund's biggest weaknesses, the lack of incentive on managers and staff to learn from experiences, especially failures, and to take risks in doing things differently. The big question about Bradlow's proposal is whether his additional elements would help more than they hinder.

---

[52] Cox bill to 106th Congress, First Session, draft dated 17 September 1999, sec. 1308, emphasis added.

Conclusion

Reform must be multidimensional. There is no one silver bullet or initiative that responds to the several legitimate concerns about the accountability of the IMF. Reform must extend beyond the composition of the Executive Board. The 'don't fight with the cook' and 'Yes, Minister' syndromes lead some to believe that Executive Directors cannot ever on their own hold staff to account. Efforts must be focused inside the organization. One priority is to diversify staff recruitment. This must precede what should also be priority efforts for more provision for outside voices – to ensure there are staff inside that will understand outside voices. Effective accountability requires facts – more 'virtuous circle' forecasts, risk analysis, monitoring and evaluation of results. There is merit in the proposal for establishing an independent think-tank in Washington to assist staff of developing countries to increase the effectiveness of their participation in the IMF. Perhaps the example of the Advisory Centre on WTO Law is a departure point for its design. In line with the view that to increase effectiveness, it is in the interest of all that more voices are heard, there is minimum downside to establishing an ombudsman. If nothing else is done, the Independent Evaluation Office should be strengthened, with an increase to its currently very modest resources.

Of the various ideas and recommendations presented, we believe highest priority should be given to modernization of quotas. Who sits at the table is of critical symbolic and substantive importance. The answer is not to increase the size of the board, nor to remove the creditor majority. The Europeans have it within their power to break the impasse. Of all the inexplicable dimensions in the IMF, the most inexplicable is the European grip on seats (6 out of 24, not counting the Spanish or Swiss constituency). The six Europeans (Belgium, France, Germany, Italy, the Netherlands and the United Kingdom) have about 30 per cent of the voting shares.

If Belgian, Dutch and Swiss actions in the IMF were consistent with their rhetoric and their well-deserved reputation for international development good works, they would unilaterally cede their quota and Executive Board seats. 'Jubilee 2000'-type lobbying and public pressure should not have to be brought to bear on Belgium the Netherlands and Switzerland to yield their Executive Board seats to more populous, bigger countries. The way forward is to redefine the quota allocation formula to target decreases for Belgium (5.14 per cent) and the Netherlands (4.85 per cent), and Switzerland (2.85 per cent), who together in sum have shares larger than China, India, Nigeria and Brazil combined. An approach can be devised to reallocate quota, with developing and emerging countries paying for their increased shares. Imagine the impact if enlightened Belgians, Dutch and Swiss took the lead.

Index